Candidate Contracts: Taking Back Our Democracy

A Step-by-Step Plan for Radical Electoral Reform and 3rd Party Empowerment

by

John Rachel

Published by
Literary Vagabond Books
Los Angeles • Osaka
literaryvagabond.com

LITERARY **LV** VAGABOND

Candidate Contracts: Taking
Back Our Democracy
Copyright © 2015
by John Rachel

Print Book ISBN #978-0-692-46601-8

Cover Art by Gregory Canton

Table of Contents

PART III

Acknowledgements

As has become my heartfelt custom, I want to thank my best friend and wife, Masumi Nishida, for her encouragement and faith in me, and her magnificent ongoing role as my teacher and guide in discovering the wonders of Japan and Japanese culture.

Incentive for writing this book came from many diverse sources within the greater conversation about the state of democracy in America and the devolution of America into a plutocracy.

While the electoral strategy I am proposing here is entirely original, this work was informed and inspired by many brilliant and dedicated individuals, whose scholarship and passion represent beacons of enlightenment and hope. I include among them: Noam Chomsky, Ralph Nader, Chris Hedges, Richard D. Wolff, Naomi Klein, David Stockman, Robert Scheer, Dennis Kucinich, Scott Baker, Ellen Brown, Paul Craig Roberts, David Swanson, Ray McGovern, David Glenn Cox, Robert Parry, Michael Collins, Kevin Zeese, Chris Floyd, Rob Kall, Robert Reich, Michael Moore, Bruce Gagnon, Patrick Walker, Marcello Rolando, Patrick Martin, Kevin Tully, John Whitehead, Timothy Gatto, Kathy Malloy, John Little, Richard Clark, Dave Lindorff, Jay Janson, Linh Dinh, Tom Engelhardt, Julian Assange, Edward Snowden, Chelsea Manning, Jeff J. Brown, Robert S. Becker, Heal Herrick, Matt Taibbi, Glen Ford, Stephen Lendman, Jim Hightower, David Corn, Glenn Greenwald, and Katrina vanden Heuvel.

A number of personal friends offered casual editorial and aesthetic advice: Travis Rood, Lance Collins, Randy Winters, Russell Swider, David Everitt-Carlson, Kathryn Rushent, Judy Rachel, George Polley, Ron Ruiz, Gilly Adkins, Oliver Lamm, Gary Clark, and Richard Stolzenthaler.

Invaluable editing suggestions were also provided by Terry Sneller.

Introductory Overview

This is a manifesto presuming the unconditional condemnation of autocracy and political corruption, the sinister dismemberment of American democracy, and the illegal disenfranchising of the vast majority of voters from the political process. It assumes that anyone picking up this work is already familiar with these very real, profound, sophisticated, highly-developed, rapidly-accelerating, internal threats to our country, in particular the assault on our unique form of democracy.

Thus, this book is not just more whining.

Lord knows, there's been enough of that.

We know what the problem is. The system of government delineated and putatively enforced by the Constitution has been hijacked. Congress is broken. When anything does make it through the gridlock, the filibusters, the showdowns and ultimatums, the lockouts and shutdowns, the grandstanding and chest beating, the trivialization and verbal mayhem that passes for debate, it only does so because it serves the interests of the corporate oligarchy, not the needs of the common citizen.

Still, let me make this perfectly clear.

This relatively short monograph is NOT more analysis, hand-wringing, lip-biting, and moaning about the *problem*.

Rather, this book is specifically what I believe we can and should *do* to address the mutilation and theft of our democracy. It is an approach tendered in the yawning dearth of viable remedies.

I will be outlining here a step-by-step plan for a full frontal assault on the corrupt and dysfunctional mess that's been made of our electoral process. We all know Citizens United and McCutcheon made politics a pay-for-play game of legalized bribery. We all know that the voice of the average voter has been drown out by a virtual tsunami of money from rich donors and multinational corporations.

Therefore, I am offering a new paradigm, an entirely new set of standards to which all politicians should and must be held to. This is not an appeal for magnanimity and cooperation. The politicos of the two major parties ABSOLUTELY WILL NOT want any part of this. If they surrender to the demands of this new paradigm, it will because they have no choice.

Based on overwhelming evidence, I see little chance they will do so.

On the other hand, I predict that minor party candidates — and as a far-left progressive I am talking about bona fide liberals and leftist independents — will happily embrace these ideas, as will voters once they understand them.

6

Here in a nutshell is what powers the strategy.

The approach is engineered to create an enormous tension, literally an irreconcilable showdown, between voters and the two major parties. It leverages that irresolvable tension into support for minor party candidates.

If implemented as outlined and the resulting glaring contrast between politics-as-usual and the new paradigm unfolds as I hope, the strategy will create a solid and enduring bond between voters and non-traditional candidates — minor party and independent, which for convenience I will henceforth call "indies", because they are independent of the prevailing two-party regime — and shatter the monopoly which the two major parties have enjoyed for far too long.

My plan provides a specific method for recruiting voters in support of a mechanism which empowers them and puts the major party sell-outs — the professional politicians who are now exclusive servants of a rich and powerful elite — on the defensive.

Massively on the defensive!

Since my proposals taken in total constitute what is an electoral strategy — a methodology designed for winning elections — much of what follows will read is as if I'm giving hard-nosed advice to individuals running for office.

That absolutely is the case. I am offering what I think are fundamental tools essential for connecting with voters and winning at the polls. This is a program for a game-changing end-run around big money politics.

My central purpose is getting enlightened, progressive-minded individuals elected, ones who listen and answer to the people who vote for them.

Of course, my browbeating indie candidates is not the whole story.

I'm talking to voters as well. Since this strategy decisively and powerfully *connects* voters to candidates, and literally creates a *legal bond* between a candidate and his or her future constituents, it is vital that all participants understand and embrace the concept and method — voters and candidates alike. Even though it is the candidates who are in the obvious position to initiate and put this strategy in play, it urgently requires that the voters commit to it as well. It requires that the people going to the polls almost unanimously expect and demand that all candidates for elected office play by these new rules.

The need for this will become apparent when the strategy is fully explained.

To be perfectly frank, I am very confident voters are going to be all over this. This is not just a set of tactical weapons to be used *on* voters. It's literally an answer to their prayers. Their voices will finally be heard loud and clear if this takes hold. It offers tools by which they can *demand* the representation they need and deserve, if *'government of the people, by the people, and for the people'* is not going to be just hollow propagandistic sloganeering masking de facto autocracy.

On the other hand, I am rather worried about the indie candidates. Why? Because political aspirants are typically cautious, afraid to try radically new ideas for fear of ridicule, and when new to the game are usually inclined to defer to the expertise of more seasoned veterans. Trust me, they will not be getting anything remotely like what I'm recommending here from established campaign consultants or other veterans of the campaign trail. The approach is extremely unconventional — entirely outside the box — and if fully implemented will be quite controversial, to put it mildly.

Because it is so unique, the strategy I am proposing requires boldness, real courage, total commitment, and major chutzpah. It is not for the timid. It is not for the equivocating. It is not for the risk-averse. It most definitely is not for anyone who is not prepared to take a lot of abuse. If my ideas work the way I intend them to, there will be a lot of very angry Democrats and Republicans with a ton of money and political hatchet men at their disposal. Things are going to get ugly fast.

From what I've observed in the past, progressives tend to error on the side of civility. They show up with a racket and shuttlecock, ready for a friendly game of badminton. They are shocked and offended when their opponents wield swords, knives, guns, howitzers.

I am all for civility, for taking the high road, maintaining dignity. These are wonderful, healthy things in a perfect world. They are to be encouraged and embraced in a world where there are rules which respect differences of opinion; promote open, intelligent, inclusive debate; value thoughtful analysis and consider verifiable facts as critical to constructive conversation.

But just look around. Politics is a gladiator sport! It increasingly resembles a game we used to play as kids — the boys did anyway — called King of the Mountain. There were no rules. Any means to knock the guy on top off and take his place was fair game. It's a good thing we didn't have hand guns back then. We would have used them!

Between the media, which reduces practically *everything* to a sporting contest, and the politicians, who have every reason to avoid a serious, substantial discussion of the real challenges facing the country, modern campaigning is all about winning, knocking the other guy off, and getting on top.

Thus anyone who is serious about being elected — even those gentle souls who are at core just decent people trying to make a positive difference — must be dressed for battle. They need to be daring, aggressive, relentless. While I'm not suggesting that indies lower themselves to the level of cage fighting barbarity that we often see in contemporary campaigning, I am saying that it's important to recognize how the game is now played and not cower inside some fantasy world thinking that voters prefer meek mild

Clark Kent. They don't. They put up with Clark only because he becomes amazing, dazzling, mighty man-of-steel Superman. Or Wonder Woman. Ready to fight to the death for what's right and good.

The media, always needing to top yesterday's blitz of scandal, gore, hysteria, confrontation, and violence, feeds the dizzying feedback loop, this whirlpool of insulting irrelevance and crass disinformation. We end up with what-bleeds-leads reporting. It's a game of one-upmanship that for democracy is a race to the bottom. Political campaigns are beauty pageants and talent shows like American Idol. Major party candidates are given a pass just repeating talking points, regurgitating sound bites, posing and strutting to push their poll numbers.

It's truly nauseating. To add insult to injury, providing voters with clear, meaningful choices is submerged by a glamour parade of photo ops and slick campaign ads. Often the media focuses on such inconsequential issues, or the differences in the policies of opposing major party candidates is so blurry, people are left with no real basis for making a decision. None whatever. They just go with their gut, or based on habit or party loyalty, stay the course and vote how they've voted in previous elections.

It gets worse. Some voters base their decision on smear ads, emotional appeal to ethnic groups and specially targeted communities. The truth doesn't factor in. Who knows what the truth is anyway?

Money plays the decisive role in this type of campaigning because it's purely a battle to get a pre-packaged message out to as many people as possible. Whether that message has any validity or is constructive, or is just a pack of lies isn't important. It's how many voters you can reach and hustle into your corral. Voters become sheep. Tell the flock whatever you have to in order to win the numbers game.

This is what we're up against.

I'm not saying that progressive indies can't hold their heads high, can't maintain their dignity, can't take the high ground. But they *are* going to have to be bold, assertive, aggressive. They're going to have to get LOUD sometimes. They're going to have to be a little mean. They're going to have to get "mad as hell and not take it anymore!" Just like the crazed but thoroughly engaging Howard Beale in the classic film *Network*.

I see some fire in people like Bernie Sanders and Elizabeth Warren. Ralph Nader held his own but didn't look like George Clooney, so the media massacred him. Jill Stein can certainly rumble some times.

If this fire-in-the-belly were just a little more prevalent on the left, I would find greater cause for hope. Unfortunately, I'm not seeing it.

Thus, I confess to sounding a bit shrill in this book. At points it may appear that I'm browbeating progressive candidates, talking to them like they're stubborn children. I get very impatient. Progressives have the most powerful and important message since the founding of America, right in their hands. Why aren't they out there fighting for it? What happened to the energy of the civil rights movement? Where is the anger and contempt for one cruel, irresponsible war after another? I have for so long — and I know many of you share these feelings — been disappointed, even infuriated, by what I see as the spinelessness and lethargy of the left. Occupy Wall Street (OWS) offered a brief glimpse of what was possible. Then it was destroyed before it got any momentum. I don't even hear any cries of outrage about this blatant oppression of free speech. People should be furious about what happened to OWS!

Obviously, I am carrying a lot of pent up frustration. Maybe my prejudices and anxieties will prove to be unfounded. I sure hope so. Time is running out.

In closing this introductory section, let me be absolutely clear about something else. This strategy is *not* for any indie candidates who have a narrow, inflexible agenda. If someone has certain pet causes he or she wants to make the entire focus of their campaign, end of story. This strategy is built around what the *voters* think is important. While saving Antarctic plankton and restoring the Caerulean Paradise flycatcher population are worthy causes, neither is what concerns *huge* majorities of American voters. Any progressive candidate serious about getting elected to office must start listening to voters and building campaign messages around the issues which the public truly cares about.

The good news is there are plenty of very important *progressive* issues where there is overwhelming consensus, agreement across the entire political spectrum. Not to marginalize any worthwhile niche causes, the plankton and flycatchers will just have to wait until we get good people in office. Those and other good and worthy concerns will be addressed in due time.

Lastly, a comment on presentation: The style here is informal. I am not writing an academic piece. That's not to say it isn't well-researched, supported, meticulously thought out, thoroughly explained. It just means that I'm more interested in writing a persuasive work than a scholarly work. I am more interested in mobilizing for action than surviving the rigors of peer review.

Regime Change Utilizing Extreme But Requisite Measures

What is being proposed here is a method towards achieving nearly a clean sweep of the legislators currently in office. There is no longer any room for compromise. We have endured decades of broken promises as America deteriorates on every front. The professional class of politicians have had ample opportunity to do the right thing. Somehow it never occurred to them that doing the right thing — that is, being sensitive to and responding decisively to the will of their constituents — was the reason they were elected to office. Good riddance to them. I am sure they will get cushy, high-paying jobs as consultants or can adapt their talents to work the comedy club circuit.

Because I believe that many current office holders are decent people and there is some remote chance of rehabilitating them, inherent in the proposed electoral strategy is an opportunity for incumbents to come around and redeem themselves. I have serious doubts that any of them will take advantage of it. But it is a genuine opportunity — even if the terms are ironclad and non-negotiable — to *begin* representing the people, and to totally and irrevocably turn their backs on their current base of puppet masters. Without question, we have ample evidence where their loyalties now lie. We see the carnage they have wrought, both the carnage of destructive and completely unnecessary wars, and the cold treacherous internment of representative democracy. We have witnessed their facilitating the transfer of wealth and power to their corporate sponsors and plutocratic masters.

To be candid, I'm not very optimistic the old guard will come around. Old habits die hard. Feeding at the corporate money trough may be too entrenched in their world view and modus operandi to imagine doing things any differently.

There clearly are a few good ones. But the vast majority of current legislators — at least 84% — can go and no one would miss them. This will especially be apparent and widely acknowledged when the public finally sees what real public service looks like.

So let me make this absolutely clear. I am dead serious about this. This short manifesto is about replacing a minimum of 450 legislators with candidates *not* affiliated with either major party, and putting an indie candidate in the presidency.

I don't see any other way to pull this country out of its death spiral, its accelerating descent into moral and financial bankruptcy, social breakdown, and total dysfunction — barring, of course, a revolution. But in view of the 300,000,000 guns now privately owned, that would be a bloody mess and probably no recognizable version of America would come out the other end.

If what I've said thus far at least intrigues you and the little voice in your head is saying …

> *"Hmm. This author might be crazy,*
> *but let's see what he has to say."*

… please read on. I promise this will not be a waste of your time.

Most importantly, please read with an open mind. Save your objections and arguments   — I suspect you *will* have many negative knee-jerk reactions along the way — till the final page. This book is not about tinkering or playing around the edges. It contains a brutal, paradigm-shifting, game-changing set of proposals. On-the-surface they may seem outrageous. But if you can get beyond how extreme they appear to be at first glance, I think you will be rewarded with an epiphany, or at the very least be armed as never before with some powerful instruments to respond to the equally brutal, paradigm-shifting, game-changing and outrageous insults this country has been subjected to by the oligarchy, the incomprehensibly rich plutocrats, who now own our political system. Their program has been devastatingly effective at massively shifting the country's wealth and power exclusively to themselves, a very tiny privileged class, in the process committing America to permanent war, inflicting misery and hopelessness on the most vulnerable in our society, gutting the middle class of opportunity, destroying for 99% of Americans any shot at the American Dream, replacing our democracy with an autocratic corporatocracy, waylaying the Constitution and its most basic protections, and fundamentally refashioning our country into a feudal police state.

If none of this bothers you, and/or you think that change is impossible and/or believe that investing your time and energy in making an epic transformation of our country is frivolous or unimportant, then certainly this book is not for you. Maybe you should read *Little Women* or *Gone With The Wind* and pine about the good old days.

To be candid, I too am sometimes daunted by what sometimes appears to be a hopeless situation. But not trying has the certainty of failure. Not listening means the deafening roar of corporate totalitarianism will be the theme song for many generations to come. Not acting is the laziest form of surrender. Not opening up to new possibilities is fatalistic complicity with stasis and inevitable collapse.

Perspective

Do I think that a successful challenge to the current electoral system — the two-party duopoly dog-and-pony-show we call democracy — will instantly solve all of our problems and put this country back on track?

Absolutely not.

I am not that naïve.

However, it is an absolutely essential part of the overall solution.

It would result in the *beginning* of a new era of politics, which will break the embargo that now exists — the boycott of meaningful citizen participation, which now totally precludes meaningful civic dialogue and debate, tramples constructive ideas and initiatives, and prevents a new vision of America from ever being aired.

It's frankly a matter of putting the horse before the carriage.

It is facing up to a fundamental reality ...

None of the crucial progressive reforms we need to implement can be achieved without direct action or support by all three branches of government.

I constantly see important, positive, comprehensive demands being issued:

- We need to get rid of Citizens United.
- We should transition America to sustainable energy.
- We must have election reform and get money out of politics.
- We have to protect the oceans and address climate change.
- We should get rid of corporate personhood.
- We have to break up the big banks.

Specific issues are targeted:

- We should give amnesty to immigrants who have lived here a long time.
- We must have minimum nutritional standards in school lunches.
- We have to stop corporations from shipping jobs overseas.
- We must increase the budgets for food-safety testing.
- We should subsidize college tuition fees.
- We have to hire more teachers.

These and dozens of great ideas are floated, as if saying them loudly and frequently will magically make them come true.

But they *all* have to become LAWS or they are just more wishful thinking.

Even sensible calls for amending the Constitution require action by legislative decree — either with a two-thirds majority vote in both the House of Representatives and the Senate, or by a constitutional convention called for by two-thirds of the State legislatures.

Frankly I'm at a loss for identifying anything of importance among all of the critical changes that must take place immediately or in the very near future, that *does not depend on passing laws*, that doesn't at the end of the day *require* action by elected officials, either legislating or enforcing them.

Either we get Congress with the support of the president and the courts behind these noble initiatives, or they will continue to be ignored and brushed aside, regardless of how much the public wants them, regardless of how many petitions and demonstrations there are, regardless of how many op eds and blogs are written, regardless of how *essential* they are.

It all begins with *forcing* our system to be truly representative.

13

It all begins with *making* our elected officials *listen*, then *act* decisively in our favor.

And that begins with a massive game-changing reshaping of electoral politics.

• • •

Let's look objectively at the state of progressivism in our country, the efforts being made to introduce progressive initiatives into the political and social arenas.

Right now there is a profusion of ideas and tactics floating around, some excellent, some just okay.

Divest from corporations which are abusing their power ... *Great!*

Boycott companies which are not friendly to the environment, forbid union membership, use child and slave labor ... *Very positive. Punish the bastards!*

Start a petition. Promote it on Facebook ... *Eh. Probably ineffective. But sure. Why not?*

Get out in the streets. Demonstrate. Hold up signs ... *Wonderful. Signs are fun. We always need to get the right messages before the public eye.*

Start a co-op. Grow food. Buy locally ... *Sounds good to me. Organic veggies!*

Ride a bicycle. Become a vegan. Meditate ... *All healthy personal choices indeed.*

Cut down on greenhouse gasses. Reduce your carbon footprint ... *No brainer. Do it!*

Pool your money. Buy an island. Live sustainably in a community of equals ... *Very noble and perfect for the fifty or so on the island.*

These and others like them are all to one degree or another productive ideas.

But the reality is, no singular approach, no two or three, or even *all* of the above in combination, no matter how noble, spirited, or well-intended, will significantly alter our current disastrous course and put America back on track.

To think otherwise is to ignore how pervasive the poisoning of our entire society is, how broad and deep the systemic corruption of our social, economic, political — especially political — institutions are.

To think otherwise is a failure of perspective and proportion.

The butterfly effect is nice for fairy tales.

But the dynamic of political and social change is hierarchical.

And it is in a society as complex as ours an almost incomprehensible order of scale.

It's not playing in a sandbox. It's trying to move a mountain.

Or maybe for our purposes here — sticking with the metaphor — it's like tunneling *through* a mountain.

Thus, while much of what we call progressive initiatives are laudable, they don't address problems or offer remedies at a level or on a scale where they can take hold and endure.

The current electoral system both installs bad people — as in narrow-minded, anti-democratic demagogues — and it massively subsidizes bad behavior — meaning that either a candidate plays by the rules of big money or he or she doesn't get elected.

If *that* state of affairs doesn't change, all hope is lost.

● ● ●

Sometimes — too often for maintaining a semblance of sanity — I ask myself ...

How did we get to this miserable place?

It couldn't have always been this bad.

Am I deluding myself?

I am 68 and I remember growing up in a much different America.

Is my memory failing me?

Am I becoming a romantic old fool, glossing over the bad, gussying up the good?

The simple answer?

No.

Looking at the cold hard facts clearly demonstrates that about 45 years ago — though the pre-planning dates it back a bit further — some dramatic changes got underway.

I don't need to go into all of it. But certain items stand out.

These are the big red flags which illustrate conclusively that as a nation we are now going backwards, and have been for some time.

- Real wages have been flat.
- We are embroiled in wars everywhere. The War On Terror has put us in a permanent state of military readiness and active conflict.
- The War On Terror is just as destructive within our borders as without. We are constantly being watched. Our local police now look like Navy Seal teams.
- The media is a homogeneous monopoly.
- The wealth of the country has migrated upwards. Wealth inequality is at a historic high.
- The top .1% now own as much as the bottom 90% of the population.
- The banks are too-big-to-fail and the bankers too-big-to-jail.
- Our manufacturing base has been gutted.

- The middle class is being slowly decimated.
- Our country is heading toward neo-feudalism.
- Our public education is in shambles. College is becoming unaffordable.
- The number of people living in poverty has doubled since 1973.
- Our country is being sold to the highest bidder and now foreign ownership of U.S. assets is at a historic high.
- We have more people in our prisons than any other major industrialized country.
- Racial tensions are back. Bigotry is becoming overt and virulent.
- People have less and less faith in their government.
- Correspondingly, the government doesn't trust the people. It spies on us. Citizens are now often regarded as guilty until proven innocent.
- On the international stage, at one time we at least appeared willing to cooperate with other nations. Now we just bully and bomb.
- Once a beacon of hope and a source of inspiration, America is increasingly feared and reviled throughout the world.

Jump right in.

Add your own favorites to the list!

How did this happen?

That's the easy part.

Our *legislators* have enabled and promoted all of this.

Laws have been written and passed.

Often the public has been lied to and misinformed about these laws.

Moreover, horrible treaties have been put into play.

The public has been lied to and misinformed about the consequences of these treaties.

How do these lies get distributed? That's easy.

The main stream media has become the propaganda arm of the U.S. government.

The clincher ...

The U.S. government is now exclusively controlled by the corporate oligarchy.

How has this gotten by us? That's also easy.

We get what and only what *they* want us to know and think.

The absence of a vibrant press challenging the official narrative and the corporate agenda of that narrative, coupled often with rigorously orchestrated *disinformation* campaigns, has rendered the American public horribly uninformed, misinformed, generally confused about public policy and national priorities, unable to make sense of any of it.

Even when the public has understood what was going on, their voices in shaping public policy have been increasingly ignored. We the people have been shut out of the process.

And on those hopeful occasions when the "good ones" — legislators like Paul Wellstone, Dennis Kucinich, Bernie Sanders, Chuck Schumer, Ted Kennedy, Sherrod Brown, Elizabeth Warren — have stood up and tried to resist any of this, they have lacked critical support from both within their own ranks and among the citizenry. While armed with good intentions, opposition to what has been driving our decline and disintegration has been weak, disorganized, incapable of fashioning a coherent and powerful message, clearly inept at mounting any kind of vigorous defense, much less proactive offense.

That having been said, here is the obvious question …

Where in this mass of confusion and defeat for progressive causes does an election strategy fit in? I know many on the left have given up. They are discouraged and disillusioned by gerrymandering, voter disenfranchisement, voter ID laws and related impediments to even getting to the polls, and the potential for outright theft of elections via fraud and tampering with electronic voting machines. They say that the electoral process is so malignant and corrupt, regardless of how much time and effort we put into it, the impact of the ballot box in achieving reform will be negligible, if not entirely lacking.

Here's what I say to that.

First, *their* methodology is clear. The plutocrats force progressives to be always on the defensive, in constant retreat, with an aggressive policy built around keeping us constantly scrambling and in disarray.

One day it's police brutality and militarization of local enforcement agencies. Then it's an attack on women's rights and abortion. Next it's secrecy and prosecution of whistleblowers. Then it's another manufactured war. A few days later, it's net neutrality and free speech. Then attacks on same-sex marriage is all over the news. Cutting Social Security and Medicare. Then it's drug testing, attacking legalization of marijuana. Then more police killings of innocent people. Mix in immigration issues. Throw in some ISIS, EBOLA, Russian aggression, Charlie Hedbo, Keystone XL, TPP, TTIP, government shutdown. While we're gasping for breath, the attack on Social Security and our pension funds revs up again. Cut unemployment benefits, cut funding for anything benefiting the poor. On and on and on it goes.

It reminds me of when I was a kid. We'd find a nice big ant hill, the little guys just going about the business of being good productive ants. Then we'd pound the center of it with a baseball bat. Instantly the entire anthill sped up ten times in a frantic jumble of activity. There seemed to be no order to it. Just ants running in every direction at once.

Well … we're the ants and the corporate-imperial oligarchs are the kid with the baseball bat. Just look at us, constantly scrambling around, not knowing what hit us, or where the fresh blow will come from next.

We can learn something from this.

We must counter that ploy by counter-attacking *them* on as many fronts as possible.

The best defense is mounting a formidable, if chaotic offense. Unpredictability conveys a huge tactical advantage.

Keep *them* guessing where they have to send the police next.

Keep *them* wondering where and what disruptive prank we might pull.

Granted, some of our efforts will only end up being annoying background noise. In fact, my frequent criticisms of many of the things done currently as protest, typically conjoined to hyped-up expectations — online petitions is a perfect example — is that they just amount to low-level static, which the powers-that-be simply ignore or merely find amusing.

But some things can and do blossom into serious challenges to the established order.

Occupy Wall Street is a perfect example of a simple protest, initially modest and not all that promising, that blew up huge, right on the doorsteps of the financial elite, and soon got *them* seriously worried. They suddenly found themselves with a big, ugly public relations problem, which rapidly evolved into their justifiable fear that the movement could go national, get out of control, and quickly grow into a large-scale insurrection. The Obama administration at the prompting of the Wall Street financial sector — the nuclear core of the 1% — did somersaults to quickly marshal the necessary resources to immediately crush the movement.

While it lasted, OWS represented a potent and effective protest.

It created the most famous meme in recent history — the 1% vs. the 99%. It's still be used hundreds of times a day in the media.

Though OWS was relatively spontaneous, it was viral and genuinely rattled the establishment.

We can only find out what will be effective by trying. Trying everything possible. Test strategies. Test tactics. Probe for vulnerabilities. Float as much as possible before the public to see what grabs its attention.

That's exactly what the oligarchs do to us.

They keep us reeling from one thing to the next.

They keep hitting us over and over.

Never letting up.

I say we give them their own medicine.

We keep *them* scrambling. 24/7/365. On every possible front. We take the fight to *them*. We fight the fight on *our* terms.

We do a lot of what we've been doing.

Only more!

We petition, we demonstrate, we rally, we attend their meetings, we pour out pamphlets, we inundate the social networks, we picket, we strike, we stand up, sit-down, fight fight fight.

Recognize that none of this will bring the empire to its knees.

But it provides a lot of aggravation and distraction.

We throw noise and chaos at *them*.

BECAUSE ...

Finally — and this may come as the biggest surprise of all, precisely because we've got them distracted with all of the other stuff — we attack them in the VOTING BOOTH.

That's right. It's so on the up-and-up, so *inside-the-box*, they won't see it coming.

Or they won't see it in time to do anything to stop it.

Strategically using the voting booth will be effective because it's so obvious, so perfectly above the board.

There is no effective defense against it. Unless they outlaw voting.

It will put them totally on the defensive, require them to expend a lot of resources to shore up and defend their fortress of deceit, their tacit and supposedly impregnable grip on the outcome of "democratic" elections.

Remember ...

The plutocrats have a lot invested psychologically and financially in maintaining the *illusion* that voting makes a difference, that we still have a one-person one-vote democracy. We'll use that duplicity *against* them. Call their bluff. Make it true by acting as if it were true.

Here's the conspicuous tactical advantage to this, one that cannot be overestimated: With OWS, *they* had the law on their side. The presence of demonstrators could easily be construed to be in violation of local ordinances. Trespassing, impeding pedestrian and vehicular traffic, marching without the proper permits, littering, loitering, causing health hazards, and so on.

What are they going to say about using the constitutionally guaranteed right to vote?

> *"Excuse me, ma'am. But I'm placing you*
> *under arrest for ... for ... VOTING!"*

Flawed and corrupt as our electoral system is in its current form, it still represents a powerful — perhaps *the* most powerful — vehicle for direct citizen impact on the system.

While recently the implementation of voting has been so tightly constricted and thoroughly contorted that it no longer produces comprehensive and fair citizen representation, the *infrastructure* for representative democracy is still in place.

The challenge is getting around and ultimately eliminating the constrictions and contortions. Making the system work the way it is supposed to.

That may seem like an impossible task. The American public has been effectively trained and brainwashed. Most voters are locked into the Democrat-or-Republican paradigm. Legitimate challenges have been marginalized. Minor parties have been demonized.

But understand that if we can't break that hammerlock on the public mind, then the only other option is …

Well, that's the problem. There is no other option.

At the same time, let me be clear. I'm not driven to embrace the impossible just because there is no other possible.

On the contrary, I am only suggesting that we may be being too hasty throwing in the towel, grossly premature deciding that formidable obstacles amount to game over and assured defeat.

I am of the opinion that it *is* still possible, using an unprecedented and unique form of leverage, to move voters beyond the duopoly paradigm and force open the electoral process.

In fact, the current sad state of our electoral system actually reinforces that view.

Seeing this just requires a different perspective.

The simple truth is that tens of millions of voters still embrace the notion that our corrupt two-party system somehow works and represents their interests. You can deride them as sheeple, dismiss them as naïve and brainwashed. But that's just taking the easy way out. It's throwing away a valuable strategic asset — a level of commitment to and faith in American democracy, however misplaced — which could prove pivotal to our struggle to reform the system.

Let me explain.

The very fact that so many still believe that our fraudulent democracy somehow works for them provides us a means to mobilize them. Their delusional embrace of the two major parties means they are at least somewhat engaged — or more important, *engageable*.

It means that at least to some degree, they are paying attention. They are *approachable*. They may be discouraged or even disgusted but haven't completely written the system off as a total loss.

If they are as riveted by the frivolous dog-and-pony show put on by the Republicans and Democrats as they seem to be every four years — nothing like a convention to show the world what a circus American electoral politics has become — they must have some grain of hope that the system will eventually deliver for them.

I look at this optimistically. Given a message which truly resonates with their needs and desires, I think there is the potential for real engagement — not just knee-jerk reflex voting — a potential that we can *flip* their loyalties.

The key is offering a message which rings loud and true.

Granted, voter participation is low and declining.

But again I take that as a *positive* sign.

The number of registered voters is not going down. In fact, despite all of the obstacles being put in place to *prevent* people from registering, citizens are still being added to the eligible voter rolls.

Here is an interesting statistic: While registration for both major political parties has suffered slight decline, new registrants designating themselves as independent rose over 11% between 2008 and 2013.

Here is my take.

While people still keep their voter registration intact, they are beginning to see the light. They are becoming increasingly disenchanted with the results. More and more voters are realizing that with the two major parties, what they see is *not* what they get. They are increasingly frustrated and now beginning to disengage, seeing voting as less and less effective. Therefore, enthusiasm for going to the polls and engaging in what is increasingly seen as a fruitless exercise is waning.

Nevertheless, and you can call it what you like — irrational, delusional, Pollyannaish — people still have *some* faith in the electoral system, which is why registration keeps increasing. Whether a habit of thinking passed down from parents, or the result of effective brainwashing in high school civics class, Americans see their country as *democratic* and elections potentially as a valid form of citizen participation.

I see America for now at a very important historical juncture.

But time is running out. Before we end up with 0% of registered voters showing up at the polls, we need to reinforce and rescue the prospect that voting can actually mean something, that voting can make a real difference. While there is still that faith in the system, we need to extend to voters a real choice, give them the hope that their voices can be heard again, offer them a fresh narrative that includes a genuine alternative to the lack of imagination, paucity of vision, and homogeneity of the two major parties.

My conclusion …

We have before us a rare opportunity to reach out and communicate our progressive message to a vast number of citizens. These are people who are still engageable, disenchanted with what they've been witnessing for the last couple decades, and hungry for something better. This is a rare opportunity to debunk what misconceptions voters have about "liberals" and the left, get them to see how much they share progressive values with most other citizens, how much they have in common with a progressive vision of America. It is an opportunity using the established channels of our flawed electoral system, to reach vast numbers of citizens who probably aren't likely to join street demonstrations, who don't sign MoveOn petitions, who won't be joining a commune in the Indian Ocean, but who still genuinely care about their country.

It is a golden but soon-to-be-lost opportunity to share our message with millions of Americans who are soon to discover how relevant and important what we have to say really is.

That is what this book is about: effectively messaging tens of millions of voters, offering them real hope that there is an alternative to the stale, ineffective, deceptive paradigm of two-party politics in America, and providing a powerful mechanism for breaking the hammerlock the two corporate parties now have on the system.

It offers a step-by-step plan toward restoring real representative democracy with the enthusiastic support of the voting public.

To put it bluntly, things are so bad we now only have two choices: Burn down the building or use the door to get in while it's still open. Meaning it's either a revolution or using what little wiggling room we still have at the polls to leverage some big changes.

At the risk of being labeled an alarmist, that wiggling room might not be the case for much longer. Signs of creeping totalitarianism continue to mount.

Summarizing …

Whether we have a real democracy or not, the powers are giving lip-service to it. They claim we still have the right to voice our choice at the polls, even if money in politics has so narrowed that choice it mocks the very idea of democracy.

I say as long as at least in theory that option — choice at the polls — still exists, lets take the plutocrats at their word and play the game. Let's call their bluff. But with a decisive difference: we'll creatively *expand* on the rules and create some *real* choice at the polls before they know what hit them.

The approach I'm laying out in great detail in this book, I believe ultimately has the potential to make each and every vote count. It will put on notice every single person running for office: Either make a firm, legally enforceable commitment to serve the interests of your future constituents or forget about getting elected.

America

America by and large is a progressive country.

This is true now and becomes more so by the day.

Whenever you poll people on most critical issues and you don't prejudice the polling by identifying a particular stance as 'progressive', don't mention the 'L' word, or God forbid say anything about 'socialism', the majority of voters get behind progressive ideas.

The most popular government program in our history is pure socialism, that program being Social Security. Despite the best efforts of the rabid right, there are still many similar forms of citizen aid and assistance which serve the greater good. All of this is enthusiastically supported by the majority of Americans, who haven't lost their sense of common decency.

Of course, you would never know this if you get all of your information from the main stream media. But that's neither here nor there. Or I should say, that's a topic for a whole other book.

What is relevant here is that the fresh new paradigm, the sledgehammer strategy being outlined here, will only be broadly applicable to progressive causes. The simple reason for this is that the strategy builds on the deep commitment Americans already have to the "general welfare", to progressive ideas whose time has come — and in fact have never left — but which are increasingly being demonized by pay-for-play politicos with the complicity of the media, a distortion mirrored in the debilitating corruption of our electoral system.

Significantly, though the strategy promotes a progressive agenda popular with the vast majority of American voters, it *cannot* be implemented by either major party. They are both far too beholden to corporate and other regressive special interests to embrace either the progressive policy commitments *or* the methodology itself. The methodology uniquely precludes a candidate who adopts it, from any possible adherence or exclusive loyalty to the corporate agenda of the plutocrats.

In summary, the approach is specifically tailored to empower *minor party* and *independent candidates* who are appealing to voters on the basis of progressive policies which are ignored or avoided in major party campaigns.

• • •

Let's explore "minor party" a bit more.

The list of minor parties currently operating is surprisingly long. Wikipedia lists 28, *plus* Libertarian Party, Green Party, and Constitution Party, which it enigmatically considers major parties. Perhaps this is because those three each have a presence in the majority of states and Washington DC. On the other hand, performance at the polls hardly supports the notion any of these three are major players.

Putting aside considerations of ideology, the Libertarian Party stands out above all other minor parties as the best organized, most pervasive third-party force in America.

But it is opposed to strong government at any level and by any measure would be considered regressive.

Putting considerations of ideology back on the table, the Green Party leads the pack in terms of organization — as loose as it is — and fights for good progressive causes. It functions nationally, meaning it can put candidates on the ballot in almost all 50 states, the importance of which is obvious but cannot be overstated.

My hope for the success of the strategy being presented here is predicated on the belief that it will be enthusiastically embraced in all national races by Green Party and independent candidates. If it works for the Justice Party or the Peace and Freedom Party, all the better. Cindy Sheehan would at least stop all the pointless wars.

But I see it as a glove fit for the Green Party and any independent candidates who align themselves with the Green party platform and Green New Deal.

Therefore, as an editorial note, I will be using a convenient acronym from this point forward.

When I refer to one of "our" guys, meaning the progressive alternative to "their" guys, who are either the Democrat or Republicans running for the same office, I will refer to him or her as the GP/I candidate.

Finally, occasionally I use 'third party' synonymously with 'minor party'. If a minor party emerges to pose a serious challenge to the two major parties, it will be a *third* major party, in the sense that it will be the third party to get in the center of the fray and have a real shot at winning.

• • •

America is at another tipping point. It has only occurred twice before, the most recent being during the Great Depression of the 1930s.

People are ready for change. People are *screaming* for change.

Voters are fed up. They are discouraged … disappointed … disenchanted.

2014 gave us one of the worst voter turnouts in our history, just over 36%.

Congress's approval rating hovers in single digits.

According to recent polling …

- 63% of voters think congressmen get reelected because elections are rigged in favor of incumbents.
- 58% of voters believe most members of Congress are willing to "sell" their vote.
- 59% voters think their *own* representative has sold his or her vote for cash or a campaign contribution.

- 63% of voters want to replace their current representative.

Of course they didn't do it.

Because they felt they had no choice. It was the incumbent or some even lower-life barbarian.

The lesser-evil phenomenon.

But let's not lose hope.

Carpe diem!

This is a very unique time we live in.

There is a historic opportunity which only comes along once a century.

Can we do it? Can we against all odds break the stranglehold of big money?

Can we free ourselves from the hammerlock of the corporate two-party duopoly?

Will our kids grow up thinking plutocracy and democracy are the same thing?

Will the great experiment of self-government fade into a distant memory?

If we care, I don't think we have a choice here.

If we don't try, we all know the answers to those questions.

And they're not the right answers.

PART I:

The strategy being offered here is entirely legal. In fact, it works within and reinforces the existing theoretical framework of our electoral system.

However, let's look objectively at the *de facto* state of that framework. Our system has been …

- undermined by the self-imposed sequester from the realities of everyday life for the everyday citizen by our millionaire-class politicians.

- infected by a self-serving and willful ignorance of the damage inflicted on the majority of Americans by plutocratic rule.

- corrupted by the revolving door between both elected and appointed government posts, and the privileged world of Wall Street, big banks, multinational corporations, the military-industrial complex, the mega-giant fossil fuel, agrichemical, and pharmaceutical industries.

- poisoned by the deluge of money pouring in as a result of the *Citizens United* and *McCutcheon* Supreme Court decisions.

Many concerned observers understandably judge that democracy in America is a lost cause. The 1% won. We the citizens lost. We no longer have a voice in our own government. Nothing can be done to reverse this catastrophe, barring a full-blown insurrection.

I stubbornly refuse to accept that.

Moreover, I suspect many of these same people who despair over the destruction of our electoral system, though they are reluctant to admit it, still harbor some subconscious hope that by using traditional channels, we can get the country back on track.

These same frustrated and dispirited denizens carry on and on, whining about the need for making the tax laws more equitable, reversing *Citizens United* with a constitutional amendment, re-regulating Wall Street, instituting *real* campaign finance reform, restricting lobbyist access, nationalizing or at least reining in the Federal Reserve. They talk about stopping TPP, stopping fracking, stopping unnecessary wars, curtailing the out-of-control Department of Homeland Security and national security agencies. They even call for a new constitutional convention.

But here's the question …

How do they expect to proceed on any of this *without* involving our current governing framework?

Every single one of these initiatives *begins* with action on the floor of either the House or the Senate. Unless they are recommending a revolution — a violent or otherwise total overthrow of the government — how will any of these admirable ideas move forward?

We can only acknowledge and accept that intrinsic to all of the desperate cries we hear for change, these calls to action by determined and well-meaning activists, *is* engaging the institutions now in place. That also means *holding accountable* those who now hold elected office.

We seem to agree on one thing. None of this will get done with the current crop of miscreants, corporate lapdogs, sniveling sycophants of the oligarchy, securely enthroned on their pedestals of power. The people we now have in Congress, even the President himself, won't solve these problems. They *are* the problem.

It hardly comes as a surprise that recent polls show approval of congress hovering in the 7-12% range, with dim prospects for significant improvement.

Of course, there's a lot of finger-pointing. The Republicans are the preferred whipping post right now, the party of 'No!' — a title they without question richly deserve. We also have the Tea Party, an easy target for snide remarks and outrage. They are a crude and surly bunch, to be sure.

But regardless of what particular spin we put on the dysfunction, bickering, gridlock, and comedy of errors we endure on a daily basis emanating from Washington DC, there is only one sensible diagnosis: We get what we deserve.

People simply have not been paying attention. Voters swallow the lies they are fed during the circuses we call campaigns, then swallow more lies and excuses until the next election cycle comes around, at which time they are fed the newest lies, fresh off the fecund assembly lines of treachery and deceit.

People should know better.

But they don't.

First and foremost, to get democracy to work, voters must somehow be convinced they should pay attention.

Actually, they do pay attention. A lot of attention. But to other things. Things which impact them personally or grab them emotionally. When videos of American citizens being beheaded are being flashed on screens all across America, they sure pay attention. When a factory in their home town gets shipped to Vietnam or China, they pay attention. When the local police are shooting unarmed citizens, they pay attention.

Mostly, people pay attention to their own families, their immediate needs.

They pay attention to their jobs, their neighborhood, maybe their community.

In terms of politics, they tend to tune out.

Who can blame them?

A lot of what the public is told is either nonsensical or insultingly stupid.

Trying to make sense of it is just too exhausting for today's overworked American.

And the sad fact is, it is this disengagement which has made the destruction of democracy and the looting of our economy such smooth sailing for the plutocracy.

> *"The tyranny of a prince in an oligarchy is not so dangerous to the public welfare as the apathy of a citizen in a democracy."* - Charles de Montesquieu

Unless we *can* and *do* engage a significant portion of the voting public, get them to pay attention, present them with ideas and programs and a vision that *does* make sense, restore their faith in the system and give them a genuine voice in the democratic process, there is zero chance of turning America around and creating a constructive and hopeful future for ourselves, our children, and our children's children.

Let me be completely candid.

I'm not *100% sure* that we can save representative democracy at this point. Maybe things have gone too far. It may be corrupt beyond repair. Maybe people are just too overwhelmed. Maybe the inertia and over-complexity of empire have gone beyond the point of no return.

But there are a few things I'm 100% certain of.

Things will not get better under the current arrangement.

A fresh paradigm and entirely new narrative is required.

Hope can only come from outside the corporate duopoly.

People can only hear and will only listen, if you talk their language, on their terms.

If independent and minor-party candidates are to have a remote chance of replacing the corrupt pay-for-play toadies of the Republican and Democratic parties, they must be willing to *go to the people*, not expect the people to come to them.

If people then are hearing what they want to hear — or at least hear something that makes sense and speaks to their concerns and priorities — they *will* pay attention.

I repeat.

People *will* pay attention.

Tragically, this last simple truth has been widely abused by the plutocrats. Thus, there is an incessant stream of propaganda and manipulative disinformation telling people what they want to hear, often claiming to address their needs. But unfortunately, this is pure propaganda and bears no relation to the truth.

So I am talking about telling people what they want to hear but being *honest* about it. Being genuine. Being real. Offering real solutions to real problems.

As is made abundantly clear further in this book, there actually is plenty of good news to go around. Honest, truthful, hopeful news. And even more on the horizon, if we put forth the effort. It's not the stuff that perpetuates the ongoing looting of our economy for the enrichment of the ruling class, so it goes unreported now. But there is good news to be shared — shared in parallel with the sharing of the enormous riches which the nation possesses and which the most powerful economy in the world produces — good prospects for all of us under a dramatically different set of rules and priorities. It's not that we're lacking the human, natural, industrial, or economic resources. It's that we're lacking the proper implementation, utilization and distribution of them.

Of that I am 100% certain!

Here's another 100% certainty for me.

This is not a truth as much as it is a belief.

If there is any chance, however remote, however daunting, however demanding, that we can turn this country around, restore the voice of the people in the political process and sanity to the course we want for the future, it *is* worth trying.

It is incumbent on us to stop the madness, and begin to think and act like a nation again, not a feudal empire. The whole idea of America, the essence of our noble experiment, is participation by all. Just to see this through and determine once and for all in the Petri dish of the real world, if it's possible to have self-rule by the 320,000,000+ of us, as diverse and individualistic as we are, makes the commitment to attempting a real representative democracy a worthy and noble effort.

It goes without saying, that we don't have representative democracy now.

Not even anything close to one. We have the silenced majority. Then we have the plutocrats, a tiny slice of rich and powerful elite, calling the shots.

In Chapter Two: *Zeitgeist*, I will jump right into the glaring discrepancies on some prominent key issues which dramatically illustrate the disconnect that exists between voters and their elected representatives. How, in poll after poll, there are things the voters say they want done, which never get done.

But like the lemmings we apparently are, we still go through the motions of pulling levers and pushing buttons in the voting booth. Fine. I

29

say we put some substance into the exercise. If *they* — meaning the people who are in power and whose power is upheld by this sham of a system — claim we still have a say in running our country, if *they* still insist that our vote counts, if *they* still insist on repeating the mantra, "government of the people, by the people, for the people" to mollify and assure us — the unruly, unwashed masses — that we do indeed have a functioning democracy, if *they* tell us we really do have a choice, I say we take them at their word. I say we call their bluff.

We'll have a say.

We'll have a voice.

We'll have a choice.

Only it won't be *their* choice.

It won't be a choice between Corporate Puppet #1 and Corporate Puppet #2.

We'll come up with our own alternatives.

We'll demonstrate in real time what a functioning democracy looks like.

We'll put forth candidates which we will know with *absolute certainty* will represent our interests if elected to office. *They* can still put up Corporate Puppet #1 and Corporate Puppet #2 for election. But in every contest, we'll also be running a People's Candidate.

Maybe this will fail. Maybe our attempt to rescue and recreate what we believe our democracy can and should be, will fall flat on its face. Maybe our People's Candidates will be framed and arrested on trumped up charges. Maybe they'll be demonized with rumors, innuendo, vicious swift boating campaigns, marginalize by a vast deluge of SuperPAC campaign ads and malignant propaganda in the corporate-owned media. Or maybe the voting machines will be rigged. Exit polls will show that our People's Candidate won with a 68% majority but mysteriously his vote count only came in at 23%. Maybe they'll even be assassinated. Disappeared into military internment facilities as alleged terrorists.

Will we have lost?

This will be a failure at the polls, yes.

But it will not be a total failure.

Because then we'll know how putrid and irredeemably corrupt the system actually is.

Then we'll know that there is truly only one solution.

Then Americans will follow in the words of Thomas Jefferson ...

> "The tree of liberty must be refreshed from time to
> time with the blood of patriots and tyrants."

... and those pitchforks will be brought out of the shed for a less calm and measured approach.

CHAPTER ONE

Genesis of a Plan

The strategy being offered here is a step-by-step, take-no-prisoners plan for defeating corrupt politicos at the polls. The idea is not a polite request. It is a demand. It uses the pen as a sledgehammer, forcing out of office duplicitous politicians who make implied, sometimes explicit, but thoroughly empty campaign promises, then when in office consistently vote against the interests of their constituents. Look around. This is destroying our country.

The idea for candidate contracts was born over three years ago, first published in a series of blogs on my personal website, prior to the 2012 election. I called them *Candidate Pledges* at the time, but now prefer to call them exactly what they are, *Candidate Contracts*. There are pros and cons for using one phrase over the other. Pledges were floating about during the 2012 presidential primaries, particularly in Iowa. I thought back then that the public might be more comfortable with the idea of a pledge. People were familiar with them from Iowa, and also from Grover Norquist's prior use of them in the form of his *No New Taxes* pledge, which he wielded like a machete to keep congressman in line behind his program of shrinking government. The disadvantage of calling it a pledge is that pledges sound like they're non-binding. The language I am proposing now assures they are ironclad. They are *legally binding contracts*. Identifying them in name as such makes it impossible for anyone to brush them aside as fluff. As will become evident, the power of the strategy being proposed here is predicated on them being both perceived and acknowledged as non-negotiable legal instruments.

My original blogs ran the gamut between rants — venting my anger and frustration — to thoughtful explication, outlining in detail my powerful strategy for defeating incumbents. Some of the language is certainly incendiary. No one can accuse me of lacking passion.

April 22, 2012:	"Trust No Incumbent"
April 28, 2012:	"Pledges: Candidate Contracts"
May 1, 2012:	"How Pledges Can Work"
May 7, 2012:	"The October Surprise"
May 8, 2012:	"Pledge: Oil Industry Subsidies"
May 11, 2012:	"Pledge: Social Security"
May 15, 2012:	"Pledge: Medicare"

The ideas presented in these blogs and a summary of the overall approach was published in OpEd Magazine as "Candidate Pledges: A Strategy For Jettisoning The Scoundrels and Restoring Representative Democracy", appearing there on May 1, 2012.

Then last year, I embedded the entire strategy in a novel, *An Unlikely Truth*, published February 17, 2014. Within the context of what I hope readers find is an engaging story — so far it has all four and five star reviews — I demonstrated exactly how the plan would work, that is, how it would be specifically implemented in a congressional campaign. The story was set in Ohio's 3rd Congressional District, which includes Dayton, Ohio, a military town hosting Wright-Patterson AFB, and the surrounding region, very conservative Midwestern farm country. I had the characters in the novel ripping the strategy apart point-by-point, arguing its merits, its risks, its potential for unseating a slick, ruthless, four-term right wing incumbent, the potential for blowback, and what attempts to dismiss or trivialize it might look like.

As it played out in a fictional context, my strategy was effective at drawing enormous attention to a Green Party candidate who had previously won only 1.7% of the votes. It was particularly instrumental in highlighting the duplicity of a sweet-talking incumbent, who had all of the usual advantages: a huge campaign chest, a great organization, excellent PR, favorable coverage by the local media, and a dazzling persona built around his picture-perfect family, his credentials as an ex-military man, his carved-of-the-gods manly good looks, and the teeth-whitened charm he used to expel huge gaseous balls of patriotic blather. Unfortunately for him, his voting record on many key issues ran contrary to the express wishes of his constituents. When pledges/contracts were presented to him expressing these wishes, he of course couldn't sign them without kissing good-bye the support of his trove of wealthy campaign donors. This gave my Green Party candidate the ammunition he needed to humiliate and defeat the incumbent.

Aah, the joys of writing a novel! Happy endings are much more accessible there.

• • •

Recently, I heard some talk floating around about the idea of using candidate contracts. Apparently, an anonymous handful of people see some potential here. That's a positive sign. But so far this talk is just a murmur. To my knowledge, no one has actually used candidate contracts to force the hand of an incumbent to comply with voter demands. To my knowledge, my take-no-prisoners approach specifically using enforceable legal instruments to drive out of office any of the corporate toadies now sitting in Congress, has yet to be tried on any scale.

Thus, politics-as-usual continues, frustration and distress remain our daily diet, we sink further into gridlock and dysfunction, the country becomes more and more divided, people throw up their hands, some tune out completely.

Disturbingly, there are no remedies in sight.

None that I can see, anyway.

In the progressive media channels and publications, there is list after list of what *needs* to be done. But there is no *plan*. There are no substantive proposals for calling out the duplicity of our elected officials, for countering the lopsided reporting of the corporate media monopoly, for diverting the constant stream of distractions and propaganda, and no way to work around the deluge of money which has effectively turned our government into a subsidiary of corporate America — all of which have turned democracy into a quaint memory of bygone days.

It is very discouraging.

Much clenching of teeth, bellyaching, daydreaming, wishlisting, talkity-talk, grunting.

No plan.

Most troublingly, voters continue to elect dangerous, duplicitous blowhards into office. They continue, counter-intuitively and apparently with self-sabotaging relish, to vote against their own interests. Election after election, they put into positions of enormous and profound political power individuals who ignore the stated will of the majority of American citizens. These "representatives" abandon the very people who elected them, openly serve the interests of a tiny elite of wealthy oligarchs, and usually get enormously wealthy in the process.

For the most part, it seems the American electorate have just resigned themselves to this. The corruption of our democracy has now become tolerated as business-as-usual.

But is this acceptance of the status quo a permanent feature now?

Is it so cemented into place that nothing will stir the voting public into taking a stand?

I've thought a lot about this. I've wondered how we got onto — and continue on — such a thoroughly self-defeating path. I've tried to finger who is to blame. It would be easy to be thoroughly cynical and just reckon that most people are sheeple — blissfully ignorant, docile, shallow, unthinking.

But that's not the conclusion I've finally come to.

American people are smart.

But they're confused.

Excuse me. But what else can we possibly expect? Subjected to a 24/7 blitz of celebrity gossip, mindless entertainment, trivial rumors and scandals, cartoonish narratives, a mind-numbing blitz of advertising, meaningless polls, frivolous surveys, every manner of sensationalism and spectacle, portrayals of every challenge facing America as sporting contests — usually a bloody cage fight — or school yard scraps, I can't imagine anything but confusion would emerge. Between the corporately-controlled mainstream media and the truth-averse political machines of the two major parties, it has become a Herculean task to make *any* sense out of our politics. The serious business of running the country has morphed a soap opera, a circus, a charade, a house of mirrors. Kept in place with the best PR spin and propaganda money can buy, the resulting muddle and pandemonium serves no constructive purpose for the general public.

However, it does facilitate a nefarious hidden agenda: to *maintain* the status quo, protect the supremacy of the wealthy elite, and leave the rest of us scrambling not even for our fair share of the pie, but for the crumbs at the bottom of the garbage can.

Yes, we are confused.

Yes, the system is broken.

But I think something can be — *must be* — done about this.

Nothing less than democracy and the future we leave our children is at stake.

Thus, the reason for this book.

This is my sincere attempt to offer a plan to *unconfuse* people, to *unbreak* our democracy.

Starting with the next chapter, I offer a concrete strategy, laid out in detail, defined, described, delineated — perhaps beaten to death. The strategy offers an end-run around the toxicity of big money in political campaigns, a fresh new paradigm and a hopeful narrative for putting the voice of the average citizen back in play.

It requests simple efforts by citizens at the local level, a commitment to talk to others in their community, starting with neighbors and friends, to spread the word, to engage in an honest but frank conversation. What needs to be said is not complex or difficult. The power of the strategy is its simplicity and directness.

This citizen-to-citizen conversation *does* require that we shut out much of the nonsense that we are constantly fed by the media. It begs us to each look in our hearts and see what is actually important, what we truly value. It demands that we put our petty differences aside, our party loyalties, our 'liberal' and 'conservative' tags, our ideological prejudices. It asks that we trust ourselves to use some common sense, that we stop listening to the pre-packaged "answers" — the talking points — being shoved down our throats by our self-proclaimed experts and spokespersons, especially the current batch of patronizing political leaders.

Starting this conversation will require a core of committed activists, both at the community and the national levels. But this is what political campaigns in theory are supposed to be doing in the first place — leading the discussion by highlighting the important issues and offering a positive vision for the future.

We will just do what comes naturally in a participatory democracy, but direct those energies in ways which are constructive and genuinely serve the needs of the majority of American citizens.

CHAPTER TWO

Zeitgeist

There is huge agreement among voters, across the entire political spectrum, on a number of highly visible, critical issues.

This consensus cuts across party affiliation, political ideology, race, class, religious and sexual preference, and includes all but the ruling elite.

I recognize that polling results are ever in flux but I doubt there have been significant enough shifts in public preferences to marginalize the following. The last time I checked:

> *72% of American voters want a federal minimum wage of $10.00 per hour or more.*

> *74% of American voters are for ending oil industry subsidies.*

> *76% of voters want a cut back on military spending.*

> *76% of voters want the U.S. completely out of Afghanistan.*

> *79% of voters want no changes in Social Security.*

> *79% of voters want no reductions in Medicare.*

> *80% of voters oppose the Citizens United Supreme Court decision, with 65% strongly opposing it.*

> *68% of voters think taxes on the wealthy should be increased.*

These are huge levels of consensus!

Let's take taxing the rich as an example.

If the voters in favor of increasing the taxes on the wealthy were evenly distributed across all of the congressional districts in the country, and all of the states of the union, legislators accommodating the stated will of their constituents would unanimously pass new tax codes guidelines.

Even if supporters of increasing the tax burden on the wealthy were concentrated, 100% by district, and 100% by state, we should still expect legislation to clear both houses — 295 for vs. 140 against in the House, 68 for and 32 against in the Senate — a veto-proof margin!

I won't insult anyone's intelligence by reviewing what has consistently played out in the real world over the past decade-and-a-half towards increasing the tax burden on the rich.

It's the same on every other issue cited above.

Just a cursory look at the new Republican federal budget proposal, at prior votes on the two onerous Ryan budget proposals, and countless others, tells an ugly story. Social Security and Medicare are still under attack, the minimum wage is stuck at pre-1960s levels, the military budget keeps going up, oil industry and other corporate welfare remains firmly in place.

Here's the grand-daddy of them all:

93% of American voters want GMO labeling of their food.

Mind you, this is not a demand to *eliminate* GMOs from food products. Just a simple request that anything which is or contains GMOs be *labeled* as such, so that buyers can make an informed choice about what they feed themselves and their families.

93%!

And we can't even get that basic law through Congress!

If 93% of the public wants something, that includes people in every single congressional district in America. Or if we accept that 7% of the districts contain no one who is for it, then we're still talking about 404 districts, meaning 404 congressman.

And we can't get a simple majority of 218 votes for something 93% of the public wants?

We couldn't get 218 votes in the House when the *Democrats* — allegedly the party representing the interests of everyday people — controlled the House?

That's absurd!

Obviously, something is seriously wrong.

As it stands, we put people in office making laws that we oppose, refusing to pass laws that we support. This is Kafkaesque, Orwellian, and contemptuous. But undeniable.

Maybe you're expecting me to now jump into the fray, join the best talking heads and erudite think tankers — a crowded and well-paid haut monde who achieve celebrity and status without ever going near anything resembling *solutions* to this destructive mess — proceed to analyze voting patterns, look at the psychology of self-sabotaging behavior, talk about filibusters and gerrymandering, get into all of the gory details about why this happens.

That's not at all what I'm interested in here. That's already been done and continues to be done *ad nauseam* by others more skilled and patient than I could ever be at probing the source, cause, dynamics, and nuances of our political dysfunction.

All I'm interested in exploring here is whether the glaring and offensive disparity between the public will and what comes out of our legislative bodies can be leveraged. Whether the public is sufficiently frustrated by and angry about being ignored and dismissed, that we can: 1) constructively engage them and change their voting behavior to help *them*, the citizenry, acquire the tools for repairing this mess, starting by passing specific favorable legislation; and 2) move the country in a better direction, more democratic and more progressive, more in line with the declared desire and expectations of the majority of citizens.

CHAPTER THREE

The Basic Tools

Let's get into the basic building blocks of the strategy.

I do this at the risk of some impatient, unimaginative skeptics declaring: "So what?"

Please bear in mind that the *basic tools* are not the *strategy*. I am not naively tossing out some quick-fix Band-Aids, then making inflated predictions of magical results. While there is some obvious intrinsic value to each of the building blocks, the *real power* is in the manner of their implementation, which will be covered in excruciating detail following this short chapter.

The *entirety of that implementation* is the strategy.

I beg you to stay with me here. This book is not that long. The incredible potential of the idea may not be immediately apparent. The effectiveness of the strategy has as much to do with psychology as it does with political science and game theory. While the overall approach has some prima facie appeal in the abstract, its true worthiness as a vehicle for profound change is manifested in the hands-on world of rough-and-tumble politics.

The entire rest of this book, following the short and simple description of the basic tools, explores the dynamics of the strategy as it is implemented and intended to operate in that real world.

Here we go.

• • •

My strategy has two simple but important actionable components.

First, there is a "petition", which functions also a voter preference poll and policy endorsement.

This accomplishes several things:

1) It heightens voter awareness and augments focus.
2) It tests the importance of an issue locally.
3) It recruits voters to become stakeholders in solving a problem.
4) It gives credence to the demands later made by the candidate contract.
5) It builds a core of potential voter support.

Using social security as an example, here is how the petition reads:

PETITION: Voter Preferences Survey and
Policy Endorsement – *Social Security*

I am a registered voter and will only vote for a candidate who will leave Social Security alone. If a candidate for public office guarantees unequivocally to fight for keeping Social Security as it currently stands, or better yet improving it, I will give that candidate my unqualified support.

An explanation of the terminology: It is called a petition, in that the signers are "petitioning" elected representatives to behave a certain way. It is also a survey because each signer is recorded in support of the proposal. It is an endorsement because it endorses a particular policy and commits the voter to pledge his or her vote in support of that policy, *specifically* to any candidate who likewise supports that policy.

Looking at it another way, it is an informal but genuine commitment to vote a certain way based on a politician's position on an issue. Obviously, it's not enforceable in any sense. But signing it captures an individual's intent — loosely a pledge — at the time of their signature. This may or may not translate into consistent behavior when in the voting booth, but it's better than nothing. It is something to build on.

Whether the voter follows through and votes consistent with his or her pledge by signing the petition depends on many factors. Critical in terms of leveraging declared support is: 1) how passionate the signers continue to feel about the issue, 2) what is done to reinforce their concern and maintain a heightened awareness about the particular issue, and 3) what courses of action are made available to act on the strength of their commitment.

The leveraging of their support is initiated with the second actionable component of the strategy.

The candidate contract is a contract between any person running for elected office and his or her future constituents. Again using social security as an example, it reads:

I, *[Name of Candidate]*, if elected to a seat in the U.S. House of Representatives, hereby commit to sponsor and vote in favor of legislation to establish a 10-year moratorium on any reductions to social security benefits, to increases of the eligibility age, or attempting any other alteration in the program as it is now configured, such as might negatively impact eligible recipients of such benefits.

I will not resist, discourage, or in any manner put up an impediment to, and in fact will publicly and on the floor of Congress actively promote, any and all legislation in support of this measure. If no other legislator comes forth to offer such a moratorium, I will create and introduce by my own initiative, within 90 days of taking office, such a legislative act for consideration by Congress.

I further understand and fully agree to the following: If I violate the above-stated terms of this pledge, I will tender on the 91st day after taking the oath of office for my legislative seat, my full and unqualified resignation from this elected position. Moreover, within one year of my resignation, I will refund all contributions made by individual donors in support of my candidacy for this office.

This entire pledge constitutes a legally binding contract between myself and that class of citizens who will be my constituents, should I win the upcoming election. In the event that I fail to perform the above-required actions, redress may be sought by those same citizens in the form of a class-action suit in a civil court of law, and I will be liable for a minimum of $10,000,000 damages for breach of contract. If I fail to resign from office due to my failure to fulfill the other requirements of this contract or similar contracts, I may be liable for an additional class-action settlement for an amount not less than $50,000,000. No portion of these specified settlements may be paid from campaign donations, PACs or SuperPACs.

I take this pledge voluntarily and with full appreciation of my responsibility to the citizens of the *[Name of Congressional District]* should they choose me as their elected representative. I accept the terms of this pledge as legally binding, and with a thorough and lucid understanding of its requirements and consequences.

Signed: _____

Date: _____

This formulation is for an individual running for House of Representatives, but it is just as applicable and can be configured for Senate races, even for president.

As you can see, it is a legally enforceable commitment on the part of the candidate to do everything possible to promote and further the legislative action specified in the contract, including but not limited to proposing specific legislation in support of the initiative. It provides severe penalties for breach of the terms of the contract.

Whatever revisions are made for specific implementation in any electoral context, it should allow no equivocation, negotiation, reinterpretation. It must be ironclad in every legal sense, such that violating its terms would represent political suicide.

• • •

So far I've mentioned these hot button issues, because they get quite constant polling numbers and have been fairly consistently in the public eye for some time:

- Raising the minimum wage.
- Ending oil industry and other corporate subsidies.
- Cutting back on military spending.
- Getting America out of Afghanistan.
- Keeping Social Security much the way it is.
- Keeping Medicare intact.
- Overturning Citizens United.
- Raising taxes on the wealthy.
- Requiring labeling of GMOs in food.

There certainly are others that may be relevant. Here are a few suggestions which should also be considered:

- Mortgage debt and home foreclosure relief.
- Guaranteeing free college education.
- Forgiving college student loans.
- Decriminalizing marijuana.
- Funding public transportation.
- De-militarizing the police and requiring body cams.

There are also important and highly-debated issues which are very specific to certain regions. Maybe things related to coal mining safety in West Virginia, to addressing homelessness in Florida and the Southwest, dealing with fracking in Pennsylvania, halting the Keystone XL pipeline in those states it would impact.

Additionally, there may be extremely important, highly volatile issues which take front and center after this book is published. A new war that breaks out. Some catastrophic breakdown of infrastructure. An epic collapse of the big banks. Water shortage. A nuclear power plant meltdown.

I don't pretend to be an expert across the entire varied political landscape of our vast country, or a psychic with clairvoyant insights about what may be grabbing the voting public's often mercurial obsessions over the coming months.

The point is that a GP/I campaign, wherever it is attempting to get a serious foothold, must know its own voters, its community, what's going on, what threats lie on the immediate horizon, what people really care about. It must be flexible and agile in responding to new hot button priorities.

This sensitivity and awareness is critical to shaping a progressive agenda which engages the voting public on its own terms. Sometimes this will perfectly align with pre-existing priorities and dearly held values for the campaign and the candidate. Sometimes it's going to require an adjustment, an adaptation to more urgent but equally progressive concerns.

The essential and foremost priority in implementing this strategy is being sensitive to, listening to, and genuinely caring about the needs of constituents. Then giving them absolute guarantees that not only they are being heard, but what they *want* to get done *will* get done.

• • •

There is one more extremely controversial, profoundly game-changing proposition I will be introducing for the candidate contracts strategy. There are no polls on this. There has been no discussion. It is a completely original concept which employs the candidate contract for maximum impact.

I will be recommending that every GP/I candidate who is serious about both addressing the enormous injustice and exploitation American citizens have had to endure for over two decades, and determined to win an upcoming election, embrace and implement this unique proposal.

I call it the *Peace Dividend*.

It is a very extreme but completely sensible and most certainly *progressive* proposition, which in one single unified stroke takes America off of its war footing, and begins to address wealth inequality, reduces the corrupting influence of money in politics, trims the military budget, backs off the power of corporations, and severs the autocratic control by the plutocrats of every aspect of our lives.

I'm going to save this proposal for last.

This is not done to be clever or create a "cliff-hanger" ending.

Frankly, the idea is so outside-the-box — some will call it outrageous — that I don't want at this initial stage to distract from the essential task of understanding how the petitions and candidate contracts can work, how they can interact with the public mind and facilitate the first serious opening of a minor-party option in the demoralizing and anti-democratic ascendancy of duopoly control.

The petition/contract strategy is absolutely critical groundwork. Neither the Republicans or the Democrats can embrace the *Peace Dividend*. It runs completely contrary to the path both major parties have taken and will continue to take this country. It can *only* be implemented by third-party candidates. I see my petition/contract strategy as the most effective way of laying the groundwork, then implementing it.

For the *Peace Dividend* to be taken seriously and not dismissed as some publicity stunt or act of desperation, there has to be some general sense among the voters that somewhere out there are some candidates genuinely speaking on behalf of the American people. Voters must have some predisposition that the threat to the major party duopoly is real and credible. That as part of a groundswell of antipathy to the major parties, there are *individuals* running for office who are on the side of the average American, there are candidates who are offering a credible alternative.

If the groundwork is soundly established by properly engaging the voting public with the petitions, then building their faith in the idea that candidate contracts can and should be required to validate a politician's candidacy, and finally convincing them that the candidate contracts will be effective at wresting control of elections and the legislative process from the corporate dominated lapdogs of the rich and powerful and placing it in the hands of GP/I electees, when the *Peace Dividend* lands with a jaw-dropping jolt never seen before in American politics, no one will be listening seriously to the moronic blather of either the pathetically inept Democrats or the virulently self-serving Republicans.

CHAPTER FOUR

The Petition

Collecting signatures is never easy. But it doesn't have to be onerous.

Getting people to sign a petition for a policy that is popular, on an issue that is important to them, is less daunting than it might seem.

The key is to be simple and direct:

"Hello! We're trying to protect Social Security."

"Hi! We want to raise the minimum wage."

"Excuse me. We'd like to get our men and women back home safely from the war."

"Hi! We believe the wealthy should pay their fair share."

People are busy. They don't want a lecture. The petition format I've presented is entirely straightforward and self-explanatory.

PETITION: Voter Preferences Survey and
Policy Endorsement – *Minimum Wage*

I am a registered voter and will only vote for a candidate who will raise the minimum wage to $15.00 per hour. If a candidate for public office guarantees unequivocally to raise the minimum wage to $15.00 per hour, I will give that candidate my unqualified support.

Similarly, soliciting online signatures should be simple and direct. A banner ...

**GMOs in foods should be labeled.
Please sign our petition.**

... then the signature form — with, of course, requests for email and phone number.

If there is a perceived need to explain the issue, especially if the explanation is lengthy and technical, link to another page. People already have *way too much* information to deal with. These issues we're focusing on are familiar to most people. We're not explaining the minute details of a nuclear non-proliferation treaty. The choices are mostly cut-and-dry. Raise the minimum wage or keep it at poverty level. Leave social security alone or mess up the most popular program in the history of the government. Leave our young people in Afghanistan to get blown up or bring them home. Raise taxes on the wealthy or let them keep skirting their patriotic duty.

Keep it simple!

• • •

By the way, potential signers of the petition may be curious about what the petitions will be used for, who will see them.

Question: *"What is this petition supposed to accomplish?*

Answer: *"If we get enough signatures, meaning there is a lot of public support here on this particular issue, the petitions will be shown to the candidates to let them know what the voters expect to get done."*

• • •

To reiterate …

People are in a hurry and don't want to be bothered with a lot of detail.

We keep the initial overture simple and sweet.

They will respond in kind.

"Raise the minimum wage? Sure. I'm for that."

"End the oil subsidies? Absolutely! Those companies make too much money already."

"Social Security is fine. They shouldn't mess with it. I'll sign it!"

Yes, it can be that easy!

Because, as I have already pointed out, there are huge majorities of Americans who already strongly support these particular ideas, there's not much selling to do. It becomes purely a numbers game. Talk to enough people, we'll get enough signatures.

What kind of numbers?

10 canvassers on the street each collecting 20 signatures a day accumulate 18,000 signatures in three months. Throw in a couple thousand more from the internet and you have some very formidable numbers.

And yes, the internet can be moderately helpful. That entirely depends on how well organized the online promotion is. Online petitions are the new "activism". Frankly, I don't put all that much stock in them. I get emailed so many appeals — 40 or more requests for my signature every week — for a wide variety of worthy causes, my head spins. Plus with only a couple exceptions, I see very little getting done *purely* from online petitioning.

But if two or five or ten thousand online signatures can be added to the pile of hard copy petitions, all the better. They can be Excelled and printed out five-to-a-page — same format as the hard copy petitions — to look more "real" than just a virtual statistic.

I picture campaign ads and posters featuring our good guy GP/I candidate standing next to a pile of signed petitions. He or she points to them.

"The people have spoken. They want an end to the wars."

18,000 signatures five-to-a-page (we leave spaces for collecting contact information) is 3,600 pages. It's a stack over a foot tall.

If you have three issues you've canvassed for, you have three foot-high stacks.

"This one is for protecting Social Security, this one for protecting
Medicare, this one is for raising the minimum wage. To show
the voters that I'm listening I have signed three contracts
[holds up contracts] guaranteeing my support when
I'm elected. I'm going to Washington DC
to do the job you want me to do."

Sure, it sounds a bit simplistic. But sometimes bold is just being straightforward. It seems that simple, forthright, unambiguous talk has become an endangered species in contemporary politics, if not entirely extinct. Let's bring it back to life …

Talk straight. Shoot straight. Get the job done.

• • •

It is critical that the petitions "hit home".

They must have strong gut-level appeal in the *locale* where signatures are being solicited.

While as I pointed out in the previous chapter, there are many issues which *nationally* have huge majorities of voters backing what would be called "progressive" solutions, there still are important variations within individual voting districts, which have to be taken into serious consideration.

If a congressional district, or even entire state, has a huge defense industry presence, a petition and candidate contract calling for reduction in defense spending is not likely to be very popular, or at least not as popular as similar initiatives in a region that is enthusiastic about alternative energy — wind farms, solar energy fields — or civilian R&D — cancer research, biotechnology. The latter ones want to see a reduction of defense spending to rechannel that money into their preferred projects. The former is understandably concerned about keeping their jobs.

Similarly, a district with many older, retired citizens is going to be much more worried about reductions in Social Security and Medicare coverage than one which hosts colleges and universities, hence has younger demographics. On the other hand, the latter region certainly would be strongly supportive of increasing the minimum wage, since many of their voting age citizens may be working at menial jobs to help pay for schooling. A region with young demographics *and* parents of college age children would certainly be enthusiastic about reducing or forgiving college loan debt.

Each region, whether a congressional district or entire state must be analyzed for its unique set of critical issues — its "hot buttons". The choice of petitions and corresponding candidate contracts must be attuned to the particular local needs, with an eye for these hot button issues, the one which garner strong support and voter enthusiasm.

Just as important as identifying the hot button issues, the voting record of the incumbent must be analyzed in detail, with careful attention given to a pattern of voting which runs against the apparent wishes of the voters.

In view of the statistics I cited before — the formidable consensuses that exist on critical issues vis-à-vis what comes out of Congress — it shouldn't be that difficult to pinpoint glaring discrepancies on several of these issues in most districts.

While most politicians talk the talk, the voting record provides the truth about whether they walk the walk.

It is axiomatic that if 70%+ of the nation wants certain things done, and these initiatives go down to defeat in Congress, someone somewhere must be voting against them, contrary to the wishes of their constituents. Congressional bills don't mysteriously defeat themselves. There are no bad fairies switching the vote tallies in the legislative chambers.

Someone — a lot of 'someones' adding up to a majority of elected representatives — is voting against the express will of the American people!

There are reasons why such glaring disparities — what voters want and what come out of legislatures — get by the voting public, though they're not good ones.

We all too often see a favorite son incumbent managing to get a 'Pass Go Collect $200' by his gullible constituents. He or she finds some contrived excuse, offers some twisted logic, puts up a Wizard of Oz smokescreen, manages to bury the treachery behind beautiful campaign rhetoric and well-crafted campaign ads. He or she kisses a lot of babies. Or sings the national anthem at little league baseball games.

Voters easily fall victim to the slick PR and glib onslaught of excuses and deceptions.

Why should this come as a surprise?

Political campaigns hire the best minds — consultants, psychologists, spin doctors, speech writers, ad men — to polish candidate images to a high gleam and keep the dazzled public in the dark.

This untruth-in-advertising is the vulnerability my approach directly targets.

The point of the petition/candidate contract strategy is to highlight in *stark and odious relief* the malfeasance and hypocrisy of elected representatives — their callously ignoring the needs and wishes of the people who voted for them and kowtowing to the demands of deep-pocketed campaign donors. The strategy focuses the attention of the public on the gap between promise and performance.

Thus I cannot overstress this point: Right from the beginning, those setting up the petition drive must be sensitive to the specific issues dear to voters *in their local region,* with exacting attention devoted to how and when their incumbent legislators voted on the wrong side of legislation addressing these same issues.

Having said that, we should acknowledge a practical reality ...

There is some trial-and-error to this process.

To eventually get it 100% right requires some investigation and flexibility in the early, preliminary stages. The committee putting together the petitions needs to check any available polling data, ask around a bit, make its best guesses, then be willing to shift emphasis and even quickly abandon a petition that begins to look like a non-starter. It might mean beginning with seven, eight, ten petition ideas, then narrowing it down and focusing on the three or four or five which show clear promise.

Understandably, trial-and-error should be kept to a minimum, to both save time and not look foolish or disorganized. There is a lot at stake with this initial phase of the strategy. Once the drive to collect signatures is full-speed ahead, the process of "focusing" the public's attention begins a long, arduous journey. There's no room for backtracking.

The petition, as stated, is more than a petition. It probes and tests the mood and level of engagement of the voting public. It determines by the number of people who sign it how much concern there is about a particular issue. It asks for a commitment, an endorsement of a position on that issue. It is a *consciousness raising* tool, the foundation for the candidate contract phase.

And just as important in terms of its contribution to a successful grass-roots campaign ...

It also asks for printed name, address, phone number, email address. Next to the signature line are spaces for these four items. Thus anyone who signs it and volunteers any or all of their contact information is making themselves available for future involvement, at bare minimum a courtesy call or text reminder. This is vitally important! Collecting signatures on the petitions creates a list of individuals who have shown interest and are apparently measurably committed to the stated purpose of the petition. We will assume these folks are receptive in some small way to further support the stated goal.

Eventually we will ask for their vote!

• • •

Let me now talk about very critical organizational aspects of the petition drive.

First and foremost ...

The petitions should be solicited by an independent public service organization.

It will be an *ad hoc* committee exclusively devoted to collecting signatures for the designated petitions.

It should be called something like *Committee on Public Policy Preferences* or *Public Policy Opinion Survey Group*.

If there is a good reason for doing so — I honestly can't think of any — it can be *affiliated* with a political party.

But this has *huge* disadvantages and makes the whole enterprise an easy target for calling foul. Right off, it creates the perception that the petitioning is partisan and politically driven. This makes whatever the "results" of the petitioning suspect, appear to be subject to bias or skewed by an agenda. Regardless of how objective and true the results turn out to be, regardless of how even-handed and scientifically pure the petitioning procedure is, having it be part of an organized political campaign thoroughly undermines its credibility and invites dismissal as a clever but transparent campaign ploy.

Moreover, if it is an open secret that the organization behind the petition is a *minor party*, it represents a certain death sentence to the entire enterprise. (See Chapter Eight: *Third Party = Third Rail*.) If, for example, the *Public Policy Opinion Survey Group* is at the outset perceived as a subcommittee of a local Green Party, it will be written off with the same broad sweep of skepticism as the Green Party already is, and will have no opportunity to work its magic.

Frankly I see no good reason to make a big deal about who is behind the petition-polling drive. Petitions come and go. The organizations doing petitioning are typically quite low profile, if not entirely anonymous. When a registered voter is approached for a signature, we're not promoting the polling organization, a particular party, or a particular candidate. We're just performing a public service. It is that service as it relates to the issues being addressed that is the focus, not the particular organization conducting the petitioning. After all, it is an *ad hoc* committee which will be disbanded after the election.

In my opinion, a simple distinct logo at the top of the survey forms with the name of the committee or group conducting the survey is sufficient.

A separate DBA should be filed by those running it, who are for the entire course of the petition drive *completely independent*. That is, they are not on any of the boards, or active members of the staff of the minor party initiating it. They certainly are not personally associated with any GP/I candidate running in the district.

If asked, the canvassers soliciting signatures can if they so choose, share how they personally vote, or even admit to membership in a particular party. But the petitions themselves, the day-to-day operation and administration of the petitioning effort, and any documentation, public or private, should not reflect any party affiliation or be traceable to key participants of any political campaign.

This is not as dishonest as it sounds. The collection of signatures on the petitions is by-and-large a public service to the entire district. By design the petitions don't favor any candidate over others, do not promote any campaign or party, certainly don't reference any particular candidate positions or party platforms. They are what they say they are: a means of getting a reading on what the public wants, and giving voters the opportunity to express their commitment to certain policy initiatives. Even if the underlying impetus is ultimately getting a GP/I candidate elected, there is nothing about the petition in and of itself which promotes this.

This bears repeating because it is so important …

The petitions are completely *separate from any campaign organization*, and collecting signatures will be performed in an impartial and thoroughly scientific manner. In point of fact — and I cannot overstress this — the overall strategy *requires* the results to accurately and objectively reflect the will of the voting public. The power of the entire strategy relies on the absolute reliability and veracity of the petitioning. If the results are skewed, it undercuts the leverage of the candidate contracts.

Because the petition drive is honorable, thorough, objective, non-partisan, and public-spirited, there is every reason to characterize the process of collecting signatures simply as an effort by local citizens to determine where voters come down on key issues within the voting district.

Were the outreach efforts of the Republicans and Democrats to have this much integrity and largesse, it would be evidence of a miracle of biblical proportions. I don't see it happening anytime soon.

• • •

What is the minimum number of petition signatures needed to make the strategy work?

Obviously, the optimum number of petition signatures is *every voter* in a given district.

While that is impossible and far from practical, we have to aim high.

"I am a registered voter and will only vote for a candidate who ..."

Yes, it is absolutely unambiguous. But ...

Working *against us* is the third-party stigma.

This will come into play when the pledge on the petition is called in with a corresponding candidate contract, and lo-and-behold, it's a GP/I who is asking for support.

People are afraid to vote third-party. The reason is simple. They typically see no chance a minor-party candidate will win. So voting for one is throwing away a vote.

Working *for us* is the concept of critical mass. There is some percentage, far below a majority but sufficient in terms of synergy, to create the *perception* of a winning proposition. It's the bandwagon effect. People see enough others on a bandwagon and they start to pile on.

What if 30,000 out of 120,000 voters in a district signed a petition?

What if 60,000 voters in a district signed three different petitions? This is followed by the loudly-trumpeted signing of the three candidate contracts associated with those petitions by a minor-party or independent candidate, *coupled with* both major party candidates *refusing* to sign the contracts.

Sound implausible?

Maybe not. For one thing, most incumbents *can't* sign contracts in favor of many popular policies addressing important key issues. Which is why they don't vote the way the public wants them to in the first place. These policies run counter to what corporations, big money interests, Wall Street and major banks want. And they are the ones funding the major party candidates. If major party candidates were to sign such candidate contracts, all their campaign contributions would dry up faster than a plate of macaroni left in the sun.

If the publicity on this is organized properly and drives home the bold independence and populist heroism of the minor-party candidate's standing up to the big-and-tough but stubborn major party candidates, the *perception* that this underdog just might win could get traction. Suddenly, the public sees it as a David vs. Goliath story. They recognize that those contracts spell out exactly what needs to get done, and here is a 'David' determined to do it. They remember how David vs. Goliath turned out!

No one knows the critical mass threshold for any given situation. But it is a real phenomenon. Advertisers depend on it heavily. Advertisements in print and visual media only accomplish so much. It's word-of-mouth and copy-cat behavior that does the heavy lifting.

I can't overemphasize this point ...

If the public's attention can be focused on the contracts and the GP/Is running for office who *do sign them*, sharply contrasted with the recalcitrant major party candidates who can't or won't sign them, there is a chance for an independent or minor party candidate to break through the election day lock out. If voters can see a direct connection between voting for a candidate — a live, breathing *individual* — and getting something done they really want done, that vote is all but in the bag.

Which is why I will later stress with almost hysterical zeal the need to *personalize* campaigns.

Voters don't vote for programs or platforms. They vote for *people*. The exception to this is straight party loyalty voting, where a Democrat or Republican pulls the lever for the entire party ticket, because that's what they've always done, and probably that's what their parents and grandparents did.

Recent statistics indicate, however, that blind party loyalty is waning quickly, as confidence in Congress and other elected bodies plunges into single digit percentages.

Confidence in Congress

■ % A "great deal" and "quite a lot" of confidence

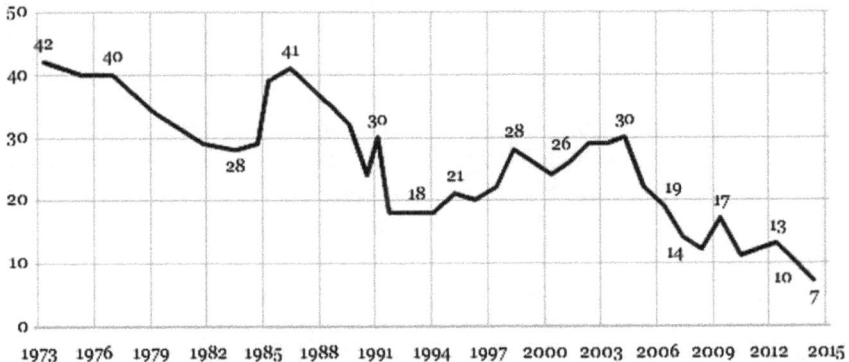

GALLUP

As I mentioned before, registration for both Democratic and Republican parties is in a slow decline, while new registrants designating themselves as independent rose over 11% between 2008 and 2013.

This is a very hopeful sign.

Unfortunately, it has not so far significantly translated into new loyalty to minor parties.

Which again calls attention to the importance of the petition drive.

The petitions engage people who have been left out of the process. They draw attention to those issues that really matter to voters.

Petitions plant a seed that is nurtured by voter frustration, which then grows into suspicion and distrust, finally becoming disdain for the major-party candidates who consistently have failed to deliver.

Voters are already beginning a slow migration away from the Democrats and Republicans.

This can only accelerate in the current climate of corporate oligarchic rule.

Voters are becoming increasingly discouraged.

Many voters are not even bothering to vote.

That is the grim reality.

But it's a reality which *can* be leveraged to advantage.

• • •

The timing of the petition drive is not exact but it is important. Starting too early means people signing them will have long forgotten about them when the candidate contracts appear. Starting too late is obviously fatal to the entire enterprise. There will not be enough time to build momentum or capitalize on progress.

For a November election, I propose starting the petition signature drive in April and going through September, maybe October if the interest is still there.

The bulk of signatures should be collected June, July and August.

July 2016 will be a month of heightened interest in politics. Both major party conventions are scheduled for the end of the month — the Republican July 18-21 in Cleveland, and the Democratic July 25-28 in Philadelphia. People will be dazzled and wowed, distracted and dumbed-down by the extravagant dog-and-pony-shows. But at least they'll be thinking politics.

Once the parties have chosen their respective presidential puppets and come out with their platforms, that may or may not prove to be an asset in August and September. It entirely depends on whether the major party platforms or the major party candidates themselves substantially address the "key" issues, the ones which are the focus of both the local and national GP/I campaigns. This especially hinges on the major themes for the presidential race, which is the biggest circus of all.

Of course, as part of the theatrics, there is always noble-sounding talk, inspired, sometimes eloquent speeches at the conventions and on the campaign trail, and vague language in the party platforms tap-dancing around the important issues. But rarely — and I think we can expect the major parties to be especially true to form this time around — is there a substantive commitment to specific solutions, e.g. *raising* the minimum wage to $15 per hour, or *increasing* Social Security benefits and *lowering* the age of eligibility, or *forgiving* all college loan debt, or direct *bailouts* for homeowners facing foreclosure.

You can bet the farm that nothing of that scale or specificity will make its way into the rhetorical jet stream of campaign blather or the hard copy of party platform propaganda.

Hopefully, the public will not be so wowed and neutralized by the histrionics of the conventions, or distracted by sensationalized attention directed to non-critical but often contentious issues — like abortion, gay marriage, immigration — that they will still be able to focus on the existential threats to the quality of their lives, sometimes even their lives themselves, and be receptive to the truly important matters the petitions identify.

We can hope. But more proactively, we can accept the enormous task and responsibility of keeping those issues front and center at every opportunity, both given and created ourselves.

CHAPTER FIVE

The Candidate Contract

Assume that the collection of signatures on the petitions is on track. Over a period of many months, using canvassers on the street, the internet, solicitations through organizations such as clubs and unions, church and community groups, professional associations, and so on, the number of people steadily grows who are "petitioning" for their desired policies and initiatives.

The next step is the *fundamental core* of the entire strategy.

The candidate contract.

Meaning …

Using candidate contracts to drive a campaign to a successful conclusion.

Defeating the Republican and Democrat opponents and putting the GP/I candidate in office!

The timing of signing and publicizing the candidate contracts, challenging the opposing candidates to sign them, then creating a major media brouhaha when they don't, is subject to a number of factors.

Initially my instincts leaned toward thinking the later the better. I originally even called for "The October Surprise", which would have been to spring the contracts on the major party candidates first week of October. I am not an expert in boots-on-the-ground campaigning, but at least back then, in the early formative stages of the strategy, I figured five plus weeks would be enough time for widespread exposure to the voting public of the GP/I's bold, game-changing gesture. Moreover, coming completely out of nowhere in the final stretch of the campaign, would catch the major parties off guard and not give them sufficient time to mount a formidable counter-campaign. I assumed such a counter-campaign would consist of the usual distortions and vituperative fictions which are the staple now of political disinformation ads — swift boating and other SuperPAC propaganda — and probably a *counter-contract*, some weak, ambiguous sham document which would allow an opponent to claim he or she too was willing to "sign on the dotted line."

An epiphany is now staring me in the face.

Actually, three epiphanies.

First, waiting until October or even the week before the election makes no difference. The major party can put out counter-attack ads overnight. They can cough up these malignant phlegm balls quicker than a lifetime smoker with lung cancer. Their bullshit machine is finely tuned and has plenty of money behind it. Better to come out early with the contract and be prepared for the inevitable deluge of deceptions and slander. If it turns into major scandal and head-to-head death match, all the better. It'll be free publicity. The candidate contracts are easy to understand and explain, so it's not impossible to win the public over regardless of how much money is thrown at maligning the concept.

Second, if a candidate contract becomes a serious threat, *of course* the major parties will come out with a null copycat version. How could we expect otherwise? Again this keeps it in the public eye and can play to our advantage. Our parry …

> *"Don't get fooled again. Read the fine print. The so-called contract by [name of opponent] is a joke. This is what we've come to expect, sad to say. Line up the broken campaign promises end-to-end and you have the limo ride to Washington DC. Please, Mr./Ms. [name of opponent], stop insulting the voters. Either sign the real thing or step aside for someone who has a legally binding agreement with the voters to do the job they want done. By the way, that's me!"*

Moreover — and I'm not doing this to tease but to make a credible claim which you can expect to see fully substantiated — the *Peace Dividend* proposal I will describe later cannot be copycatted. It is so extreme that no watered-down version can possibly be invented by the major parties. There will be *no false equivalent* of this. Trust me. So the timing of its announcement should be based on optimizing its exposure and impact.

Lastly, with the existing antipathy by the media toward anything other than the *"tight race between the Democrat and Republican"* an onerous fact of life, we need as much time as possible to push the candidate contracts out to the public.

If they do get serious traction early, the expected firestorm of controversy and disinformation from the major parties will actually *help* to keep them in the public eye for the long haul. The effrontery and sheer audacity of requiring candidates to sign a contract — because they simply *can't be trusted* — will keep the whole controversy alive and prevent it suffering from burn out. The longer the dispute rages on, whether about the legitimacy of the candidate contracts themselves or the phony versions which major party candidates will certainly come up with, the longer the public will be hearing and talking about them, the greater the chance that people will take them seriously, and they more likely voters will discover how empowering they are.

While I would leave the timing decision to individual GP/I campaign teams, I am leaning now toward coming out in August, early September at the very latest with the contract challenge. This is primarily to capitalize on the heightened public interest and awareness stirred by the coming conventions, capitalizing on whatever comes out of those circuses as kindling for local and ultimately national campaigns.

Let me offer examples.

We have a GP/I candidate running in a young, working class district. His appeal …

> *"The Democratic Party platform calls for relief from low wage poverty. The Republican platform promises promotion of good paying jobs. That's all very nice. But here is a contract <u>guaranteeing</u> legislation for raising the minimum wage to $15 per hour. I signed it. Will [name of Democrat opponent] sign it? Will [name of Republican opponent]? I put it in writing. This is what the voters here say they want. So I signed on the dotted line."*

We have GP/I senatorial candidates running in Maine, Vermont, West Virginia, New Hampshire, Florida, Connecticut, and Pennsylvania. These seven states now boast a median age of their populations of over 40. Let's say signatures on petitions in those states hover at 12-15% of the registered voters. The message of the GP/I senatorial candidates in those states …

> *"The Democratic platform says protecting Social Security is a priority. The Republican platform vaguely talks about making life good for retirees. Here is a contract guaranteeing legislation for <u>raising</u> Social Security benefits by 10% to 15%, indexing future benefits directly to inflation, and lowering the eligibility age for full benefits to 62. I signed it. Will [name of Democrat opponent] sign it? Will [name of Republican opponent]? I put it in writing. This is what the voters here say they want. So I signed a legally binding contract."*

This comes out two months before election day.

58

Before the presidential debates.

It this does catch fire, guess what will be the hot topic in the debates?

And if it's not mentioned in the debates, everyone will be asking why!

You can see that my thinking about timing has evolved quite a bit since I first came up with the plan.

I am now of the opinion we need to play it safe and come out early. Let's be honest. It may take a little bit of time for the word to get out and about. The media is a big problem. Since it's a minor party candidate in the driver seat on the contracts, getting attention from the big news rooms, at least at first, will be an uphill battle.

But once main stream media gets wind of what will play as a "hot new twist", of something completely unexpected and out of left field, something new and definitely unusual, I think in terms of media coverage we might have a game-changer.

Maybe candidate contracts don't bleed. But they can still lead.

It's taking something good for "the general welfare", something genuinely supportive of true democracy, a significant and substantial contribution to the otherwise redacted and lame national conversation, and turning it into something of a spectacle. If this upsets candidates from the two major parties, we are a long way towards being taken seriously.

I hate to be so blunt: But we need to make the major parties feel some pain.

Grown men and women crying on TV makes great news programming.

CHAPTER SIX

No Time for Half-Measures or Politeness

Make no mistake about it. This strategy is not polite. It is not nuanced.

The time for polite gestures and halfway measures is long past.

For decades we tried pretty please. We've bent over backwards, negotiated in good faith, cooperated and compromised. We listened to excuses, doubletalk, sometimes outright obfuscation. We accepted their postponements, promises, apologies at face value.

We even idiotically thanked them for trying so hard.

To see what we got, just look around.

Just look at the mess this country is in.

Look at how badly the majority of Americans are getting screwed!

So ...

This strategy is about coercion.

It is a sledgehammer approach which brooks no compromise or wiggle room, entertains no tinkering or adjustments, is not subject to debate.

It draws issue by issue a bold line in the sand, an ultimatum.

Either would-be elected public servants fully comply or it's game over for them.

We threaten the politicos with the one thing they understand — their job security.

In doing so, it forces our elected representatives to do what they should be doing in the first place. Or it's bye-bye.

When we hire a plumber to come over and fix the pipes, we don't leave it up to him to do what he feels like doing, what he's in the mood for. We certainly don't expect him to come in and sneakily sabotage the garbage disposal because he's getting a kickback from a supplier on the other side of town. There's an estimate, a contract. The job gets done right.

Even with other professionals — doctors, dentists, attorneys — we have *some* certainty about the services we expect them to perform. Usually it is something in writing.

It's peculiar, when you think about it, that we have up to this point "trusted" our elected officials, based on a smile, handshake, vacuous slogans and empty promises on yard signs and bumper stickers, to do the right thing.

To varying degrees that has worked over the years.

But sorry, folks. It doesn't work anymore. (See Chapter Fourteen: *The Honor System.*)

Something has gone missing now for quite some time — integrity.

Now we have to fill that dangerous gap with something substantial and ironclad.

Legally binding, fully enforceable candidate contracts fill the bill.

• • •

Let me be clear.

We're not doing this to be mean.

We're doing this because it is the right thing to do.

It's democracy in action.

Plain and simple.

In a way, it's a lot like making a child do his or her homework by threatening to take away their bike, their favorite computer game, or television privileges.

The ultimatum contained in this strategy is equally straightforward: Either represent us by voting the way we, your constituency, want, or we take away your job.

The contracts draw a clear line in the sand. It's *their* choice.

But since *they* — the Republican and Democratic lapdogs of the corporate oligarchy currently holding office — cannot sign the contracts, we *will* take away their jobs.

We the people will line up at the polls and elect GP/I candidate of *our* choosing, not the bought-and-paid-for stooges of the Koch brothers, Sheldon Adelson, the oinky pigs behind Karl Roves American Crossroads, or any of the other corporate oligarchs.

• • •

To be blunt about it, nothing else has worked.

We are doing this now because we have no choice.

We didn't choose the treachery, gridlock, malfeasance.

In our own naive and optimistic way, we have patiently tried to work with our elected officials. We've bent over backwards to accommodate them. We've listened to their hollow blather while the country has been plundered by Wall Street investment banks; while corporations have shipped our jobs overseas; while oligarchs have *bought* our democracy right out from under us; while the country has been lied into horrible pointless war after war; while wealth inequality has made America look more and more like a Third World country; while the 1% *refuses* to pay their fair share in taxes to the nation that made them incomprehensibly rich; while corporate lackeys installed into elected office by a tsunami of money have mismanaged the economy and squandered hundreds of billions of tax payer money on foolishness; while opportunities for the youth of America have dwindled to nothing, such that after assuming massive debts for a college education, all that awaits them is a job at Walmart or McDonalds. We trusted these fools and they pay us back by *spying on us*, treating *us* like we're the enemy, militarizing the police, criminalizing free speech. We try to politely raise a few objections, and they beat us, arrest us, shoot unarmed American citizens dead in the streets for jaywalking or selling a cigarette. Due to the gross neglect of our infrastructure, our bridges are falling down, our roads are falling apart. Due to a Neanderthal view of foreign relations, we are now considered the greatest threat to peace by much of the rest of the world. The country is plunging toward bankruptcy because we are in a permanent state of war purely to fill the coffers of the military-industrial complex.

None of this was *our* choice.

Finally our patience has run out.

Our gullibility has run its course.

It is on *them* that *they* have forced us to take a stand.

The ultimatum we are delivering is our last-gasp attempt at survival.

It is a final, necessary, desperate gambit to try to save America from total ruin.

No matter how they will try to spin it, this idea of forcing the hands of our corrupt politicians and their plutocratic masters, is not born out of malice or a need for revenge.

It is not class warfare.

It is not spite.

It is born out of faith in an America we see being lost.

It is the highest form of patriotism.

It is the greatest tribute and honor we can show our Founding Fathers.

It is the truest expression of reverence for the America we believe in.

So PLEASE … don't ever waste time thinking or talking about *us* being surly or harsh.

Don't ever get timid and squeamish about holding any of these traitors responsible.

Don't even think about hesitating to call out any Republican or Democrat who played a role in creating this mess.

And don't worry about putting them out of a job.

They can write their memoirs or go on a reality show.

Or join the circus.

Everyone loves dancing elephants

Braying donkeys are hilarious.

The kids will love it!

CHAPTER SEVEN

Progressive Values: Broad Strokes

The way things now stand — public perceptions and expectations being what they currently are — the only thing an independent or third-party candidate offers to a voter that a major party candidate does not, is a 100% guarantee he or she will lose the election. There is nothing else which so definitively sets an indie apart.

Sure, indies make well-intended and admirable stands on many important issues. But those are deemed irrelevant — or not worth giving any serious thought to — by the certain knowledge that the candidate will not get into office. So what difference does it make?

The candidate contract has the power to put the GP/I candidate in a class entirely by him or herself, set apart from the duopoly candidates. If implemented correctly, it doesn't merely make him or her relevant, but makes the GP/I's running for office a welcome relief, even a necessity, in the eyes of the voters.

It puts the GP/I candidate *in the game* in a way which counts — that is, in a manner which has the potential to attract huge voter support. It has the power to confer to the candidate much-needed credibility, which translates to voter support in the voting booth.

The credibility and support grow out of certitude. If a GP/I candidate can *guarantee* he or she will do something that a voter feels passionate about, something the duopoly candidates *cannot* guarantee will get done, that is a compelling incentive for the voter to take that candidate seriously, in spite of not being a Democrat or Republican.

The whole idea revolves around creating a profound and vital change in voter perceptions, flipping their preconceptions and expectations from "that candidate can't win" to "maybe this candidate can win after all!"

• • •

The strategy requires making a lot of noise.
There is no room for shyness or understatement.
It has to arrive like the infantry and keep on charging.
Keep on the attack!
There's no reason to be daunted.
Creating shock and awe should not be all that difficult.

First off, the whole idea of candidate contracts is so off-the-wall, it will certainly get some initial media attention. Novelty drives the news. If orchestrated properly, candidate contracts will be the lead story for at least a couple days. After all, it sets up a *personal* confrontation with each of the major party candidates. Their integrity and commitment are being challenged by some upstart minor-party troublemaker. Lots of soap opera potential there.

On the other hand, keeping it from being reduced to a one-off novelty news item — immediately disappearing from the ADHD newscast radar screens — will require a lot of relentless pressure and concerted effort. To keep the "story" alive, the duopoly candidates will have to be challenged, pressured, harangued, *harassed*, at every public event, on every possible occasion.

Are you going to sign the contract on Social Security?

Why haven't you signed the contract on fair taxes?

Our men and women in uniform are dying!
Will you sign the contract to bring them home?

People are starving! Are you going to sign the
contract to raise the minimum wage to $15?

Here's a pen. Sign the contract to stop corporate
welfare. We need the money for schools!

But this raises something that has concerned me for a long time, a matter pivotal to the success of the strategy.

Yes, we need to make noise.

But we need to make the *right kind* of noise.

If there is anything which defines the penchant of the left for self-sabotage, it is the inability to *listen* to others outside their narrow little world, then see the big picture.

I respect the passion.

I respect the focus.

I respect the arcane devotion.

I respect the individualism and strength of purpose.

I respect the fact that someone takes the time to care about things which are certainly important but sometimes far out of the mainstream of public awareness.

Looking at the range of causes which in sum represent the cornucopia of progressive concerns and campaigns is to reflect on a truly breathtaking and ennobling range of enterprises.

But — and please forgive the horrible pun — 99% of the public DO NOT give a hoot about the spotted owl.

Why haven't you signed the contract to protect the sea otter habitat?

Here's a pen. Sign the contract to stop the cruel harvesting of shark fins!

I'm not trying to be smart-mouthed here.

I'm not making fun of worthy causes.

I'm not denigrating efforts at saving sea otters or protecting sharks.

I'm just trying to make a point.

If it isn't obvious to you, the reader, that these last two messages just do not cut it with the general public, maybe you should try to get your money back from the bookstore where you got this book.

I am trying here to appeal to common sense. I am making the simple point that though many causes in the greater scheme of things have *enormous value*, they don't result in compelling messages.

They don't speak to the desperate needs of the voting public.

They don't address the day-to-day struggle most people endure just to attempt a decent life.

They won't get *our guys* elected.

If a GP/I candidate is going to have any remote chance of sitting in Congress or the White House, the front-and-center campaign messages must *resonate* with substantial majorities of voters.

People are hurting.

People are frustrated.

People are angry and feel powerless.

People are struggling with great difficulty just making ends meet, keeping a roof over their heads and food on the table, trying to send their kids to college.

Is it right and fair for *anyone* who calls themselves a *true progressive* to ignore the real needs of people who are crying out for basic relief, who just want a fair shot, justice, respect, a decent job, a proper education, decent retirement, some minimum amount of health care?

If we as progressives don't listen to the people, what's our plan?

How should we go about attracting the attention of the voting public?

What's the strategy?

Putting out more pamphlets about how we should give peace a chance? Holding a tree-planting party? Putting up posters of an endangered tree squirrel and hoping people think it's cute? Give a Powerpoint presentation on melting ice caps?

Let's be real here. Political campaigning is now three parts circus to one part thoughtful communication. For an indie to refuse to address issues which are dear to the voting public is three parts suicide and one part irresponsibility.

The issues dear to the public I've been talking about are ones which any humane, compassionate, concerned, morally responsible leftist should be able to get behind: less war, fair taxes on the rich, a living wage, decent income and sufficient medical care in retirement years, ending corporate giveaways, reducing wealth inequality, fewer kids coming back in body bags, a shot at a good education regardless of income level, good-paying jobs.

Yes, climate change is one of the most important challenges of our times. Yes, we should respect the rights of women, minorities, GLBTs. Yes, we should have freedom of speech and worship.

But … these are not the things most people are talking about.

Excluding the issues which the fanatical right uses as truncheons for stirring public outrage and setting Americans against one another — gay marriage, immigration, Muslims, terrorist threats — what most people seem to be concerned about are their pocketbooks, overall quality of life, and avoiding death.

They want their fair share of the pie, they don't want to be cheated out of their money, they want to be able to go to a doctor and get treatment when they need it, they don't want to starve to death, they don't want their sons and daughters killed in senseless wars, they want to retire blissfully and not have to worry about making it to their next pension check. This is not an exhaustive list but you get the idea.

The concerns of the average citizen are neither trivial nor abstract. They comprise what day-to-day, month-after-month, year-after-year, defines their hopes, drives their choices, and is the source of their persistent anxieties.

This is not some bleeding-heart rant.

I don't have Mother Theresa posters on my wall.

It's right in the Constitution!

Promote the *general welfare*.

Yet, more than any time in recent history, that constitutional commitment — that unambiguous MANDATE to "promote the general welfare" — is being blatantly ignored.

What more noble task is there than to return decisively to fulfilling that promise?

What is more progressive, responsible and democratic than enabling *all* Americans on their own terms to share in the enormous wealth and opportunity of our nation and have a voice in shaping its future?

• • •

As a last desperate argument to indie candidates for employing the petition/contract strategy, let me simply ask: What have you got to lose? Continuing on the current course is a sure path to marginalization and defeat. Why should a voter "throw away" their vote on you?

> *"You've got great ideas but since you'll never get elected, regardless of how much I admire your effort and would love to see your ideas implemented, it's all just wishful thinking, eh?"*

This is a harsh reality to have to face. But as it stands, that's the way things are.

I don't see any other proposal out there which represents a real game-changer.

I hear a lot of "more of the same only more".

That's fine. As I suggested before, we have to keep *them* busy, keep *them* guessing.

But I still see it as noise on the fringe.

I have yet to encounter anywhere — and I read all of the lefty blogs and magazines — what could be called a CORE STRATEGY, one which represents an overwhelming and decisive assault on the center of power.

Of course, I've heard calls from the extreme fringe for a revolution.

But that's not going to happen. At least for now.

So what are the alternatives?

Give me *one* alternative and I'll fall into a dead faint.

There is nothing to lose here and everything to gain.

There is only one way to take on the plutocrats.

Call *their* bluff.

They say we have democracy.

Alright, let's take them at their word.

They claim we have choice.

Great! We'll have choice.

Only not *their* choice.

We'll put up our own choices.

We'll put up our own candidates.

They say we can trust them.

Fine. We'll trust anyone who puts it in writing.

They'll be condescending and brush off the candidate contracts.

Excellent! Let them wonder what happened when no one votes for *their* bought-and-paid-for lapdogs.

Let them puzzle and fret when no one votes for *their* candidates because they wouldn't sign on the dotted line and give the voting public an absolute solid guarantee that the bullshit games were over, that the people who show up in our legislative bodies will actually listen to and represent *the people*.

This is a genuine opportunity to take a stand.

A GP/I candidate has nothing to lose in showing the good, deserving citizens of this country what taking a stand looks like.

A politician that listens to and cares about *the people*?

Really?

Yes, really.

It's been way too long.

• • •

Let me make something else very clear.

This is of utmost importance.

I do not expect any GP/I candidate to misrepresent their ideas, to give lip-service to a policy just to attract voters, to deviate from his or her principles and beliefs.

I am not suggesting that a GP/I candidate *abandon* any ideals or commitments.

I am only recommending that: 1) a GP/I candidate embrace more *popular* progressive stands *consistent* with their own dearly cherished priorities; 2) that they defer to the voting public's sense of priorities, out of respect for their future constituents and the obligations inherent in the office they are seeking, again in ways *consistent* with their personally held values; and 3) be willing to *postpone* some of their favorite causes until they get into office and have successfully tackled the problems that their constituents believe are more pressing.

It comes down to a GP/I candidate *expanding* his or her understanding of the entire framework within which their own special priorities exist. Concern for the habitat of an owl or beaver is simultaneously concern for the habitat of the humans who coexist with the animals. Wanting to protect forests is an expression of values which respect humankind's place in the entire ecological environment. It is not contradictory or inconsistent to care about preventing the extinction of animal species and to care about preventing the extinction of the human species.

I hope that GP/I candidates who are inspired to attempt a position of political power, so they can address specific conditions of the planet, will

68

realize that such concerns are embraced by the larger framework of solving the challenges of the human condition.

To put it in plain English: Caring is a good thing. Caring about minimum wage and retirement benefits is caring of a good sort. If that type of caring can get GP/I candidates in a position of power, then they can do all sorts of caring and make positive changes across the board — they can both stop the wars on people and stop the wars on our environment. They can turn down the heat on the less fortunate and turn down the temperature of the planet.

None of these are incompatible. In fact, they complement and reinforce one another.

I don't see anything bad coming of this.

I see enormous potential for personal growth as well.

Listening to what the voters have to say, what is important to them, is just as important as *telling them* what they should care about.

We can all learn from one another and build a better future.

But first things first.

Let's get people back on their feet.

Let's get representative democracy working again.

Let's get the country back on track.

Then the sky will be the limit …

Renewable energy, sustainable communities, no more wars on one another, no more wars on the planet or other species.

It all starts with getting good people elected.

Let me quote from very early in this book …

> *What is being proposed here is a method towards achieving nearly a clean sweep of the legislators currently in office. There is no longer any room for compromise.*

We must at minimum replace over 450 congressman and senators, *and* the president, with individuals *not* affiliated with either major party.

It's a tall order but Americans are fed up with the way things are.

The time has never been — and may not be for a very long time — better for sweeping, radical changes.

There is every reason to put aside the countless, annoying, often petty differences, which splinter the progressive movement into ineffectual pieces. There is every reason to unite behind the reasonable and humane demands of the majority of decent Americans.

CHAPTER EIGHT

Third Party = Third Rail

Let's have an adult conversation here.

I don't know what things look like from inside a third-party campaign.

I know what it looks like from out here.

The Green Party — and I am truly, deeply committed to everything they stand for — puts out noble sentiments. They offer great ideas, intelligently-crafted and earnestly-presented, naively believing that voters deeply care about the environment, justice, human rights, etc.

Maybe they do.

Maybe they don't.

Let's give people the benefit of the doubt. Let's say the vast majority of the voting public is concerned about climate change. They think that over the course of the next 20 to 50 years we are plunging headlong toward a catastrophe of apocalyptic proportions.

There are two reasons this will make no difference in the voting booth.

First, care or not, people are scrambling to take care of day-to-day necessities. As much as they are concerned about species extinction, what monopolizes almost every waking moment are very obvious immediate threats to them and their families: keeping their car running, making credit card payments, job security, figuring out how to put their kids through college. If they're on the lower end of the socio-economic ladder, they might be worried about simple survival, putting food on the table, keeping their kids from getting shot, keeping themselves and their family members out of jail. On the slightly higher end, people worry about the value of their homes, about not losing everything when the next economic crash occurs, keeping their IRA intact, keeping their home and community safe, how to pay off their kids' student loans.

If a candidate is going to connect with voters, he or she MUST talk the language of the voters, not the language of policy papers and party platforms.

Second, being a minor party candidate is in the mind of most voters one step above having leprosy.

I'm sorry to be the one to break it to all of you well-meaning, heart-in-the-right-places GP/I candidates. But the MSM in lockstep with the two major parties have been 100% effective at marginalizing you and creating the public perception — actually an unfounded, illogical, entirely unfair *certainty* — that third-party candidates *cannot* win.

This is not a minor obstacle. This is a death sentence hanging over any GP/I campaign.

Third parties are the third rail of politics.

Period!

By the way, I voted for Ralph Nader in two presidential elections. I voted for Jill Stein this last election. I did so unwaveringly. I even had two friendships dissolve because Democrats I personally knew blamed Nader for the 2000 presidential fiasco. I didn't then nor do I now buy the unsupportable arguments blaming him for being the spoiler in Florida.

But I'm hardly your typical voter.

A lot of people still buy into that myth. And many of them have since retreated from their flirtation with third-party voting. Look at the numbers. The Green Party is going backwards.

So ... what do we do?

I see only one way to tackle this.

Elect people, not parties.

In fact, this must be the centerpiece of a GP/I campaign.

We must eschew the onerous, clunky, self-sabotaging modus operandi of party campaigning. Openly. Aggressively.

Focus on the person, not the party.

I'm not talking deception, I'm talking emphasis.

But not a subtle emphasis. A huge, overwhelming emphasis!

Let me illustrate using dialogue, say between a reporter and a GP/I candidate, who is running on the Green Party ticket for Congress:

Reporter: *"So you're the Green Party candidate?"*

BEWARE!

This is a 'When-did-you-stop-beating-your wife?' question intended to pigeon-hole the candidate, then hang a big *Minor-Party Loser* sign above the one on his butt that says *Kick Me*.

Candidate: *"Look. I don't have $5.6 million like my Republican opponent. I don't get bags full of money from the RNC. I don't have $4.8 million like my Democratic opponent. The DNC isn't shoveling PAC and SuperPAC money into my account. I get my money from the people. They send me what they can afford. $5. $10. We appreciate every little bit they can spare. Because each donation is someone saying, 'I believe in you.' So you can twist it all you want. I'm the people's candidate. I am here because of the people. I am here for the people. I am here to serve and only answer to the people."*

71

Reporter: *"But you are running on the Green Party ticket. We can safely assume you embrace its policies, accept its official platform? You answer to the people running it?"*

Candidate: *"I am running for Congress. If the voters choose me as their elected representative, I will represent them. My loyalty is directly to the people of this district. The Green Party put me on the ballot. Of course, I'm incredibly grateful for that. They have a wonderfully efficient organization and are set up in every state in the union. And I admire, respect and agree with everything they stand for. Any truly patriotic American would. Having said that, I don't answer to anyone except the people who will be electing me. No one else tells me what to do or how to do it. Putting me in Congress cuts through all of the red tape and bureaucracy of major party politics. All that back door stuff that has made the whole system grind to a halt. It's me and the people. I listen to the voters and do what they want. That's the whole problem now. Maybe some Democrat wants to get something done but 'the party' says no. That might offend some corporate donor. Or Wall Street won't like that. I'm the Main Street candidate. No middleman. No political games."*

Doesn't this make sense?

The major parties have achieved their own version of credibility, with their elaborate, ridiculously overblown conventions, platform fights, lofty speeches, extravagant but mostly irrelevant dog-and-pony shows. People watch and listen, but a deep cynicism has taken hold. Nobody takes any of this seriously anymore.

How many people hang on the edge of their seats waiting to see the platform of either major party? Does anyone sit there with a pen and legal pad getting ready to write down point-by-point what either the Democrats or Republicans claim they stand for?

So why would they worry about all of the wonderful things the Green Party or the Progressive Enlightenment Party or any other fringe party believes in? Especially since they give minor parties a snowball's chance in hell of winning.

The truth is that despite all of the official stuff that goes on at the major party conventions, despite the efforts of the main stream media to exploit every twist and turn of the unfolding drama, most people are focused on the "personalities", the candidates who are jockeying for the spotlight. Voters watch the conventions to see *who* is going to come out on top, not what the official platform is.

With the major parties, "brand" does come into play — see Chapter Thirteen: *Branding* — because many people have longstanding major-party affiliation. So a Republican, even one who is fed up with a lot of what the Republicans are doing, will watch to see what the prospects are for the Republican candidates in the upcoming election. Same with the Democrats.

I still stand by my conclusion.

Even with major party campaigns, the focus is on *individuals*.

Who is running for president?

Who is his choice for vice-president?

Who is running for Congress in the local district?

Who is running for Senate?

For better or worse, politics has become celebrity watching.

Campaigns have become beauty pageants.

Elections have become talent shows.

Bill Clinton played a mean sax.

George W. was a top-of-the-line ventriloquist dummy.

Obama is the best stand-up comedian ever to hold high office.

Politicos are manufactured rock stars in a reality show we call politics.

Something to think about.

Remember …

I'm just the messenger.

• • •

"So why are you running on the Green Party ticket?"

You don't get some reporter asking why a Republican senatorial candidate is running as a Republican.

When it comes up for a minor-party candidate, there's a reason. And it's a lousy one.

For a Green Party candidate attempting any office, I guarantee that subsequent questions will be loaded with the following words and phrases: Ralph Nader, spoiler, socialist, no chance, impossible, throwing away votes, Florida, Ralph Nader, and of course, Ralph Nader.

There is no winning this sort of verbal assault. It is designed purely to discredit the campaign.

Later in the book, I get a little deeper into reframing and controlling the narrative, dodging bullets, the whole business of morphing inappropriate or annoying questions into something useful and positive.

For now I'll stick to the point I am now trying to make.

The GP/I campaign must emphasize, must prioritize, must relentlessly push the idea that the voters are casting their vote for this *person*. Party affiliation is not important. This *person* has struck a deal directly with the voters, this *person* has put down in writing his or her obligations in the form of a legally binding contract. This *person* doesn't need anyone else's approval to show up in Washington DC and do the job he or she was elected to do.

Maybe this advice seems counter-intuitive within the framework of a party organization.

Maybe it runs contrary to the long-term program of building a presence or creating a bottom-up grass-roots organizational base.

Please remember this.

The only reason anyone would now vote for a GP/I candidate is because that *individual* can deliver something which neither major party candidate can deliver.

This *something* is of enormous and immediate value to the voter.

This *something* alleviates some onerous impediment to a decent life.

This *something* removes anxiety and misery of the day-to-day struggle.

This *something* opens up possibilities for improvements in the business of living.

This *something* takes the pressure off and promises better days ahead.

And the Republican candidate and Democratic candidate *cannot* deliver.

This may be a bitter pill to swallow.

But it *is* the current reality.

• • •

Let's take this a step further.

Let's talk about values.

I'm guessing that the reason we should care about the environment, as an example, is that we want to hand off a world which is survivable and hospitable to future generations. Trees and whales and owls are great. We should protect them and nourish the entire habitat of the planet to foster a harmonious and sustainable future for all species. But ultimately, it does come down to human beings, doesn't it? To *our* place in the scheme of things.

The course we are on now is certain annihilation. There will be no survivors. Half of the life in the ocean has disappeared in the past 25 years, we've passed 4 of 9 irreversible tipping points in terms of greenhouse gases, etc.

Why do we care?

Because we want our children and their children to live.

It inevitably comes down to people.

Having said that, let's look at some other gloomy facts of life.

74

Despite the phony glowing economic numbers embedded in the fairy tales of the current administration, America is hurting. Many Americans are hurting.

Is it such a stretch to care about the things that are important to people *right now*, so that we create the opportunity to care about longer range, more difficult to appreciate threats next year and over the next few decades?

It's still caring about people.

If the current crop of corporate malefactors — and I *do* lump all of them together, Democrat and Republican alike — are left in power, there will be no tomorrow.

Is that the way to honor the values which the Green Party and other progressives hold so dear?

There is no time to rehabilitate the image third parties now are shackled with.

There is no time to educate the public about the greater values of planet and unity.

There is no time to explain the need for a paradigm shift and systemic reform.

There is no ear for the message of a Green Party or any other progressive party or movement.

But that can turn around in a flash.

If my strategy of electing individuals with certain *right ideas* and values — who by the way happen to be members of the Green Party or like-minded independents — is successful, then *instantly* you have the perfect platform to create fresh in everyone's mind exactly what elected GP/I office holders ultimately stand for, what they intend to accomplish both in the short and the long term.

You have the perfect *team* in place to get the right things done.

Can you GP/I candidates out there *see* how this can work?

As soon as you arrive on Capitol Hill and the White House, you newly-elected GP/I office holders get right to work fulfilling the terms of the candidate contracts you have signed. You tackle the things you were elected to do. Which are in their own right and on their own terms *good progressive things to do!*

Then, as a united political bloc you direct and conduct the new national conversation. You offer a new, fresh narrative. You establish a new modus operandi — genuinely change the way Washington DC does business. You adopt more constructive paradigms. You reorient the national priorities. All of this is done in concert with and with the full knowledge of the citizenry.

There will be full transparency and the people will be roundly encouraged to participate.

You will actually have an open and honest relationship with the people who put you in office.

OMG! What a concept!

The American people will then get to see before their very eyes *exactly* what you stand for. They will get it! They will finally understand what you've been talking about all these years in the oppressive shadows of a media boycott.

On the other hand — and I regret having to be so bleak …

If you *don't* get into power, it's not just a disaster for the Green Party and other cells of the progressive movement.

It's a catastrophe for all of America.

It's an epic disaster for the entire world!

• • •

This is a chilling bucket of reality for all of you well-intending, good, decent, progressive independent and minor-party candidates out there, who are selflessly investing your time and energy to create a better world.

Maybe you didn't bargain for this.

But when you're poring over all those time-tested losing strategies that guarantee to keep you at single-digit percentages of voters on election day, think about the responsibility you have on your shoulders this coming election.

Until you win, we all lose.

Until people *think* you can win, you will lose.

Until *you* give voters a reason to vote for you, you will lose.

Specific advice to Green Party candidates: If you run on party, you will lose.

The Green Party in particular has been stigmatized. Perhaps because Ralph Nader through decades of inspiring service, an impressive record of successes in standing up to corporations, then mounting an intelligent and powerful campaign in 2000, was judged to be a serious and credible threat, he was targeted for a vicious, coordinated campaign of character assassination. The collateral damage of that ruthless smear campaign was the Green Party itself. It's now the "spoiler party." Despite it's admirable and visionary party platform — perhaps the only coherent and workable plan for saving the country — it has been effectively neutered on the political stage.

So, GP candidates, listen up — for your own survival!

If you run as THE GREEN PARTY candidate, you most definitely will lose.

However …

If you run as an *individual*, a member of your community, an American citizen who truly cares and is willing to take on the Big Boys and stand up for the American people, a *person* who is listening to what's important to *people*, you at least have a shot at winning.

Again keep in mind, I am proposing no deception here.

None.

I am not saying that anyone should hide the fact they're running on the Green Party ticket.

I am not asking anyone who embraces the values of the Green Party to twist or gussy up or abandon those values, certainly not to embrace any new values which are inconsistent with those core principles.

I am saying that fundamentally this is a people-to-people process. It's one person talking to another person about what's important and what should be done. It's one person talking to many people who share the same obstacles to a secure and decent life for themselves and their families. It's one person talking to future constituents and letting them know that not only are you listening, you will guarantee them results.

Not because it's in your party platform or among the bulleted items at the party website.

But because *you* personally care and are there to represent them.

Because as an *individual* … it's the right thing to do.

• • •

As much as the prospects for success of a untested strategy can be "proved", let me offer one last powerful chunk of support for my approach.

Let's go back to 1992.

I hate to rub it in, but even the obnoxious and barely articulate Ross Perot got 18.9% of the popular vote.

Maybe I should correct that. Perot *was* articulate. But like a truck driver. Still, he *connected* with a lot of voters. They sensed his concern, they felt his passion. Maybe that simple, stocker-at-Home-Depot style he had made people feel he was one of them.

Whatever.

Ross Perot did not run on the ticket for an established party.

He created a political movement from scratch!

His campaign machine had no prior record, no reputation, no baggage, nothing.

There is a critical lesson here.

The startling truth is that someone like him, delivering an unambiguous, simple, appealing message got an impressive number of voters to pull the lever for him.

Almost 1/5 of American voters thought this poorly qualified, former IBM salesman with a good head for business but no experience in electoral politics, should be *President of the United States*.

Simply because he gave them straight talk about what was important to them.

It can be done. Perot did it!

Of course, his temperament and erratic off-again/on-again campaign eventually undid him.

But in spite of that, he *still* got 18.9% of the popular vote.

People believed him and believed *he* would deliver on his promises.

A clear powerful message coupled with a personal signature on a number of popularly supported candidate contracts will bring in the votes for each *individual* running for office.

Maybe down the road as the campaign season unfolds, there will be enough independent and Green Party candidates who have been *personally* embraced by their future constituents, the national polls will start to show that indeed, something big is starting to happen. Maybe even the thick-headed talking heads will connect the dots and begin to report that a "third-party insurrection" is underway. Maybe at that point, the Green Party will start to benefit from some long-overdue good press and be taken seriously.

But at the outset, the key — and I apologize for beating this into the ground, but the point is *so important* — is a direct connection between each *person* running for office and their future constituents, unfiltered and unrestricted by talk of party or movement or organization.

Build electoral success one candidate at a time.

The rest will fall in place.

CHAPTER NINE

Sloganeering

As I've been arguing, the entire public face of the GP/I's campaign should be built around the candidate contracts. The contracts are what distinguishes the GP/I from the major party opponents. It sets in high relief a fundamental difference.

The Democrat and Republican *say* they will do something.

The GP/I *will* do something. He or she is legally bound!

The contracts identify what the candidate stands for, why the public should vote for him or her.

Yes, there should be an in-depth explanation of *all* of the GP/I's ideas and vision for a greater America. It should be available online and in campaign literature. Honest answers to sincere questions are the best policy all around.

But when I say 'public face', I am talking about the broad brush strokes, the PR which is the first thing — unfortunately sometimes the only thing — a voter sees.

It's the name big and bold on the can. *Aunt Sylvia's Best Peaches.*

It's right there in giant letters on the bag. *Doritos - Sour Cream and Onion.*

It's the trailer for the movie.

It's the blurb on the book cover.

It's the *most important thing* a voter can know about the GP/I candidate.

Hi! I'm Margie Marple.
I will go to Washington and protect Social Security!
You can count on it. I signed on the dotted line.
Yes, I signed a legal contract to do what
you, the voters, want done!

• • •

Messaging is a science.

At the same time, we are in uncharted territory here.

This is an untested strategy, so we need to gather the best minds of the progressive left.

We need imagination, creativity, enthusiasm, and commitment to get the message out.

I don't pretend to be a public relations expert. I can only come up with suggestions.

I mostly rely on basic common sense.

To me the appropriate approach seems entirely obvious.

The *key* to successfully engaging the public and gaining their trust is to *highlight* in stark, unmistakable relief the fundamental difference between voting for a GP/I and voting for the major party blowhards.

"There are campaign promises that blow away in the wind and then there are words on paper that actually mean something. I have signed a legally binding contract which demands that I do exactly what YOU tell me you want me to do!"

"I'm your contract employee. I will go to Washington DC and get the job done, so help me God!"

"Talk is cheap. Anyone can make promises. Had enough cheap talk? I signed a legally binding contract with YOU, my future constituents!"

"Worried about Social Security? You should be! Our current congressman voted to cut it. Which is why I signed a legally binding contract with YOU, the voters, to go Washington DC and increase Social Security benefits!"

"Say one thing, do another. Tired of the same ol' same ol'? I know I am. That's why I put it in writing. I signed on on the dotted line. I have no choice but to do the right thing as your congressman."

Campaign promises are about as trustworthy as an alligator in a baby crib. That's why I personally signed this contract, which requires me to go to Washington DC and get the wealthy to start paying their fair share in taxes!"

"My opponents talk a good story. But I signed a legal contract to go to Washington DC and raise the minimum wage to $15.00 per hour."

We can't be afraid of this. Granted it's not genteel, it's not polite. But it's the truth!

Why mince words? The Democrats and Republicans don't.

And they won't!

If these contracts start to catch on fire, believe me, the heavy artillery will come out of the shed. It'll be a gruesome bloody war on any GP/I candidate who *dares* to threaten their electoral hegemony. The incumbent will be especially ruthless. After all, his or her job security is being threatened.

Be forewarned ...

Holding back will only result in a worse drubbing.

And as the saying goes, the best defense is a good offense.

Make it personal ...

> *"Come on, Mr. [name] and Ms. [name]! If you're serious about serving the fine voters of this district, let's see you sign on the dotted line. Here, you can even use the pen I used to sign the contracts."*

> *"Mr. [name] and Ms. [name] say they support our troops. That's a beautiful sentiment for sure. But how about keeping them alive? How about returning them safely to their families and friends. I think that's an even more beautiful sentiment! So Mr. [name] and Ms. [name], my opponents in this campaign, I challenge you to sign a binding contract that requires you to vote to bring our brave soldiers home safely. I don't make mere promises. I give guarantees. I am bound by a legal contract to bring our troops home from Syria. [... or Ukraine ... or ... fill in the blank!]"*

> *"This is a simple choice, my friends. Either believe in the good fairy or believe what you see here in writing. This is the contract. These are my marching orders directly from you, the voters. I <u>will</u> <u>fight</u> the good fight for Medicare. If my Democratic and Republican opponents are serious about making Medicare even better, let's see them sign <u>this</u> contract. Let's see them put it in writing."*

> *"Are you tired of stupid wars? Are you tired of all of the waste in the Department of Defense? Are you tired of seeing the hard earned dollars you pay in taxes thrown down the drain? There's only one way to make sure the job*

81

gets done. This contract says you <u>demand</u> I go to DC and clean up the mess. And I will. Will my opponents, Mr. [name] and Ms. [name], sign a legally binding contract like this? I doubt it."

• • •

In case somehow I haven't made it abundantly clear, let me summarize.

The contracts are not something to be tucked away in the corner of a GP/I candidate's home page. They are a big deal! They are the *real* deal! They are the only thing that *truly* and *dramatically* sets the GP/I apart from the major party goons. Considering how invisible and easily forgotten minor party candidates typically are, something this drastic, bold and dramatic is required. Unless you can put up a campaign sign on the moon visible from Earth, or get Jesus Christ to come back and give His personal endorsement, *this* is it. I see nothing else out there which promises to do the job.

Give it your best shot.

Candidate contracts, front and center!

No hesitation! No fear!

Besides …

The shot that will truly be heard around the world is yet to come.

This is the *Peace Dividend* proposal coming up in Part II — please don't look ahead — which opens the floodgates for reforms across the board: Reeling in the military, addressing income inequality, fixing our broken tax system, reining in corporations, getting the country out of the clutches of Wall Street and big banks, finally introducing *honest-to-goodness* campaign finance reform.

The *Peace Dividend* is a proposal indemnified by a candidate contract, which will implement something that has never been tried in the entire history of the country.

But please understand — or at least take on faith for now: For the *Peace Dividend* strategy to work requires cementing in the public mind a confidence in the candidate contracts and faith in those who are willing to bring these powerful instruments to the political stage.

The candidate contract is the foundation for building the ultimate bridge to the voting public and completely changing the narrative.

CHAPTER TEN

Getting the Word Out

One of the first things I hear when I talk about my strategy is:

*"It's a great idea but without a billion
dollars, it's dead in the water."*

I'm not going to claim that a billion dollars wouldn't come in handy and give a GP/I candidate's campaign a nice shot in the arm.

The reality is money, at least at the outset, is a big problem.

Regardless, the message has to get out there.

Well, it can. When you don't have money, there's still imagination, energy, people, time.

A lot can be done for free or practically nothing. A lot!

Don't underestimate the power of the internet properly used, of course.

Viral videos get tens of millions of hits. It's not just kids, either. A good video will capture the attention of all ages. I've seen it myself on Facebook.

It requires being flexible, fun, different, unafraid, willing to experiment, willing to fail.

Willing to succeed!

Picture this …

A candidate is sitting holding the cutest kitten in the world! He says:

*"My son says if I show you this cute kitten, my
video will go viral. Well, I don't know about you
but I think Pixie here is about as cute as it gets!
But you know what? Some families are so poor
they can't afford to feed their kids, much less a
kitten. They work two jobs for slave wages and
are still starving. I want to raise the minimum
wage to $15 per hour. I even signed a contract.
That's what I'm going to work for when I get to
Washington. [Cut to front of mansion] My
opponent, who lives here, thinks people and
kittens don't deserve a living wage. I frankly
don't know what to say. Are people really that
selfish? [Close-up of candidate petting kitten]
What do you think, Pixie?"*

That would sure piss some people off in the campaign headquarters of the incumbent. How dare you draw attention to the incumbent's $3 million mansion!

Maybe the video would go viral. Maybe not.

But guess what? It's free!

T-shirts also cost very little.

So you have t-shirts printed ...

> *Why won't [incumbent's name] sign the*
> *contract protecting my social security?*

You put them on a bunch of darling old people. Maybe they're in a convalescent home, or having a picnic at a park. They wave and smile at the camera. Maybe they're holding kittens!

Cut to GP/I walking among them.

> *"Well, Mr. [incumbent's name] can't sign it.*
> *Because his rich donor friends want to take*
> *Social Security away. They say 'privatize' it. But*
> *that's fancy talk for taking the money and*
> *gambling it in the stock market. These folks here*
> *deserve better. [Holding up contract] That's why*
> *I signed this contract. It says I have to go to*
> *Washington and do what's right for all of you."*

Hugs and kisses all around. Free kittens for everyone! (Okay, I got carried away there.)

Or we have a video of old people in a hospital. Some are in bed, some in wheelchairs. Their t-shirts say ...

> *Why won't [incumbent's name] sign*
> *the contract expanding Medicare?*
> *I deserve to be healthy.*

How about going to a V.A. hospital? Have the amputees and PTSD victims wear t-shirts that say ...

> *Stop these stupid wars!*
> *Please sign the contract*
> *to bring our troops home*
> *from Afghanistan!*

… or whatever country we're fighting at the time. Invite the press. Shame them into coming and showing some respect for our war veterans. Then tell them about the *one candidate* who has signed on the dotted line and will do the job. The candidate who will keep America strong by keeping its young people *alive*. Final shot of vets holding a sign …

[GP/I candidate's name] signed on the
dotted line! He/she will bring our young
men and women in uniform home
safe and in one piece!

How about another YouTube video …
Our GP/I candidate is seen holding a roll of toilet paper.

Campaign promises and toilet paper?
They pretty much end up the same.

[Cut to toilet paper being flushed
down a toilet … cut back to GP/I
holding up candidate contract]

That's why I signed this! I will go
to Washington DC and make sure
the wealthy start paying their fair
share of taxes. I signed on the
dotted line!

This kind of thing is free. Shoot it on an iPhone or a Galaxy. Post it on the internet.

If it goes viral, print up some posters and t-shirts. No text. Just a roll of toilet paper and a picture of the incumbent below it. People will think it's funny and will definitely get the message.

Once this kind of messaging gets started, if it captures attention and is "different" or even "weird" enough, it'll get people talking. Word of mouth costs *nothing* and is *priceless!*

I personally hate the fact that politics, news, practically everything in contemporary life has been so completely trivialized and reduced to entertainment. But it's a fact of life. To use my *least* favorite phrase: IT IS WHAT IT IS.

Since there's no turning the clock back, it's better to accept it and use it to best advantage. In its own frivolous way, the digital revolution has at least one phenomenal upside.

And it's this …

If you have something to say and say it with some imagination and humor, the simple truth is, there's no better time than now to get free publicity. There are so many social sites, text and video blogs, blog talk radio shows, and countless other new exciting ways of spreading the word.

And it's all free!

A billion dollars would be nice. But there are alternatives.

It just takes time, creativity, a minimum of social media and internet savvy, and effort.

The world is your digital oyster.

CHAPTER ELEVEN

Messaging

Everything has changed in the past ten or fifteen years.

Which is why elections now go to the highest bidder.

People are glued to their TVs like drooling zombies and if you spend a few million on campaign ads which are almost indistinguishable from car and hair care product ads, bingo! Mesmerized voters go to the polls and via post-hypnotic suggestion, robotically vote for candidates wholly owned by the plutocrats, then return home to see the foreclosure sign being posted in front of their homes and their cars being repossessed by the mega-banks who funded the campaign ads for the guy they just voted for.

•••

Okay ...

Fortunately, I exaggerate.

While recently over 80% of elections in the Senate and over 90% of elections in the House have gone to the candidate who spends the most money, hope is not lost.

The simple truth is that new media provides opportunities for exposure and messaging which is much more powerful than television.

Occupy Wall Street had no advertising budget.

Occupy Wall Street had smart phones, Facebook, YouTube and Twitter.

Occupy Wall Street created the *most viral meme* in recent history!

The 1% vs. the 99%.

Now *there's* a message everyone can relate to!

What was Mitt Romney's slogan? I can't remember it. Maybe you can ... sort of.

Believe In America!

Wow ... really creative, eh?

$844.6 million spent to tell America to believe in itself. And he lost.

$0 to tell 99% of Americans they're getting screwed by the 1%.

They're still saying it.

That's what they believe in.

What about police violence?

The outrage about police brutality has spread like wildfire in recent months.

Did this happen as a result of $800 million worth of advertising?

Obviously, the news media has been all over the story. But the public fury over the abuse of police power, the gunning down of innocent citizens, started with smart phone videos posted on public sites.

No production crews.

No focus groups.

No teams of psychologists and public relations experts shaping messages.

No organizations, corporations, committees, or any other institutional structures.

Just raw footage of appalling behavior by trusted public servants.

The simple point is that if there is something worth looking at or reading or hearing about, something which *connects* with the public's concerns, now more than ever there are incredibly effective avenues for getting the word out.

The most important thing is to use these vehicles *on their own terms.*

No, the *Gettysburg Address* wouldn't go viral these days.

Attention spans are too short.

Social media is not about the extensive and thorough.

It's about the short and sweet. The raw and engaging. Sometimes the shock and awe.

I'm not about to attempt to offer a short course here on social media messaging.

I am only saying this: Take it for what it is. Use it well on its own terms, and it will serve well the campaign of any credible GP/I candidate who understands his or her future constituents, and most importantly, can guarantee honest, faithful representation they can't get elsewhere.

If a GP/I candidate has something worth listening to, people will listen and then tell their friends.

Using short, punchy, direct messages, embedding photos or videos and using YouTube and Instagram links, social media platforms are all you need to compete with the big advertising dollars of the major parties.

You don't think you can get a powerful message within the 140 character limit of Twitter? I got this message off the internet. It had hundreds of thousands of favorites and retweets …

@IvanBoreltzin #Ukraine
#Maidan neo-Nazis from Kiev
just killed my neighbor and his
three children.

You don't need political analysis by Charles Krauthammer or tedious pseudo-reporting from Wolf Blitzer to get the idea what happened here.

My point is that social media can be extremely valuable but it has to be used with a full appreciation of the context it functions in.

Having violated this rule time and time again myself, I know with certainty that no matter how interesting and well-conceived deep exchanges of ideas are, regardless of their intellectual vigor and intrinsic value, heady dialogue and incisive, thought-provoking debate are anathema to Facebook, Twitter, Pinterest, Reddit, Tumblr, YouTube, Google+.

Here as another example is a minimum wage idea that just popped into my head ...

> *[GP/I candidate in car at drive-up window of McDonald's] "Personally, I wouldn't want to work here. But if I did, I sure wouldn't slave away in front of a vat of boiling grease for $8.00 an hour. You shouldn't have to either. Which is why [picks up candidate contract off of passenger seat] I signed this legal contract with you the voter. When I go to Washington DC, it requires me to fight for a minimum wage of $15 per hour."*

• • •

Let's talk about negative ads.

The ad with the kitten some might even call negative.

"Some families are so poor they can't afford to feed their kids, much less a kitten ... My opponent, who lives here [in a mansion], thinks people and kittens don't deserve a living wage ... Are people really that selfish?

Negative?

I would call it truthful.

Some would say it's stooping to the level of the scumbags. Playing on heart strings.

I frankly don't think that *anyone* who is trying to put meals on the tables of starving children, or keeping old people from having to live their retirement years in some piss-smelly hellhole, someone trying to shake loose some of the $40 trillion the ultra-rich have stashed away in secret accounts in order to put people back to work and jump-start our lumbering economy, or trying to make these same über-wealthy to pay their share in taxes, could *possibly* stoop to the level that the current legislators have.

In fact, I would have no problem doing an ad which pointed out how insensitive, inhumane, self-righteous and hypocritical many of our current elected officials truly are.

The truth isn't always pretty. But it's still the truth.

Some would say blunt ads are impolite, uncivil, rude.

I will concede that they are blunt, provocative.

Actually, I'll go further than that.

I'd say they're merciless.

What does merciless mean?

It means showing no mercy.

No forgiveness. Cutting no slack.

It doesn't mean vicious, vindictive, cruel, dishonest, sadistic.

It means boldly and judiciously calling the legislators and their puppet masters out for promoting a *sick* agenda.

Why should we give these politicians any forgiveness?

Why should we be polite and cut them *any* slack?

They are complicit in high crimes against their fellow man. They are abetting injustice and gross negligence. They are robbing people of their lives, their dreams. They are killing people with profit-driven wars. They are destroying families and communities to save a few bucks on production by moving our jobs overseas.

I am appalled at how the current crop of so-called liberals give such an easy pass to the sociopaths and their representatives in our government.

"Well, gosh. They're rich. They have a different world view. They see things differently."

Charles Manson saw things differently too. We didn't sit down over latte and discuss our philosophical differences. We isolated the psychotic creep before he could hack more people up.

We sure didn't make excuses and point at him timidly saying, *'You know, Charlie there means well, but he sometimes gets a little off track.'*

Call a spade a spade.

Something else that both horrifies and baffles me is how people can be so casual about the slaughter being done in our names as citizens of this country.

"Well, I'll be darned. We killed over a million people in the Iraq War.
Hey, sweetheart! What are you making? That smells great!
Are we having my favorite meat loaf for dinner?"

I know in my heart most Americans don't mean to be this callous.

The only reason they can ignore the piles of corpses, the children, grandmothers, innocent people of every shape, size and color, is they *don't see them.*

The only reason our corrupt congressman keep getting reelected is we *don't see* and *don't face* the truth about their treachery. There is so much distraction and outright obfuscation in the news, so much drama and avoidance of earnest reporting, it's hard to know who is doing what and why they're doing it.

The GP/I candidates *must* tell it like it is.

The representatives in office don't merely have a *difference of opinion* with the people who elected them or the GP/I candidates who are challenging them.

They have fierce loyalties to deep-pocketed donors, and the average citizen is not in the equation. The current batch of elected officials bow down to the might of the dollar and those who have bought our government. The rest of us are irrelevant.

It's not one person one vote. It's big money calls the shots. It's not government by the people. It's government by big spenders. It's not government for the people. It's profits over people. Wars are not fought for honor. They're fought to fill the coffers of the weapons makers. We're not trimming programs which benefit the middle class and the needy because prudent fiscal policy requires it. We're doing it because the oligarchs don't know when enough is enough and they will plunder the riches of our nation until they breathe their last breath.

GP/I candidates, if you don't do anything else in this crazy game, this winner-takes-all war of words, at least … TELL IT LIKE IT IS!

Use the abundantly rich new media we have at our fingertips to expose the hypocrites in office, in no uncertain terms, for the traitors they are. Flush out these bought-and-paid-for politicos who are exclusively serving the wealthy, who are complicit in taking our country apart, outsourcing our economy, and destroying our democracy. No fear! No compromise!

And *please* don't ever talk to me about not being polite and gentle, about this kind of truth-telling being uncivil and merciless, when one out of four children in our incomprehensibly rich country lives in poverty.

Don't hold any truth hostage to squeamishness or some silly sense of propriety in a country that sends its youth to be slaughtered in pointless, unnecessary wars.

I didn't create the current environment.

You didn't create it.

It is what it is because greed and selfishness know no limits.

It is what it is because we can't expect restraint from the plutocrats.

This will sound like class warfare but I'm going to say it anyway.

The plutocrats are not like you, me, our neighbors.

The ultra rich are not like us!

No matter how you skew it, massage it, soften it, sugarcoat it, spin it, these .1% folks are selfish, insatiable pigs. They understandably would have us believe otherwise. But we must judge them by their deeds, not their self-serving, self-absolving, self-congratulatory hype.

Yes, they have a different world view. Here it is …

"It's all mine. Screw everybody else."

Am I exaggerating? Read Ayn Rand's *The Fountainhead* and *Atlas Shrugged*.

Look at the Walton family. This one family is worth more than the 125,000,000 on the bottom of America's economic ladder. One family! And they refuse to pay their employees a living wage. Or give them decent benefits.

The Koch brothers together are worth more than $104 billion! If you were to spend *one million dollars a day*, it would take 284 years to go through their colossal fortune. But that's not enough for them. They are buying elections so they can make *even more money!*

The people who are taking America down the path of ruin are not merciful people.

They are selfish.

They are heartless.

They are ruthless.

We must meet their ruthlessness with unshakeable determination.

We must be willing to fight.

Sometimes it won't be pretty.

Or polite.

Or civil.

I often think the left, with their obsessive "correctness", political and otherwise, is irredeemably out of touch with reality. They live so in fear of being "negative" they surrender the fight before it begins, thereby opening the floodgates for the *real* negativity.

To call some one out on their lies is not negativity.

Their lies are the negativity.

To point to selfishness and greed is not negativity.

The selfishness and greed are the negativity.

To call a warmonger a warmonger is not negativity.

The sacrifice of innocent lives in unnecessary wars is the negativity.

And that negativity will continue to spread and infect every facet of the public domain, every corner of our private lives, until it is stopped.

Pointing at a lying, hypocritical, self-aggrandizing, self-enriching lapdog of the corporate oligarchy, a politician in the pockets of the plutocrats who puts his job security ahead of the interests of his constituents, and saying, *'This man is corrupt and he is bad for our country!'* is not negative.

It tells people what they need to know so they can stop the disease before it spreads.

Anyone who enters politics because they think its a gentleman's sport where there are polite rules of engagement is naive and maybe doesn't belong in the game.

Again, I don't like any of this.

You don't like any of this.

It's an ugly reality.

But the game will not change unless *we* get into it and change it.

You cannot shame the shameless into being nicer.

Being nice to them only invites their disdain and mockery.

You can only get rid of them and replace them with decent people.

Maybe then politics will then become a wholesome, respected, higher calling.

Wouldn't that be a miracle?

CHAPTER TWELVE

Nuance Is Death!

Maybe a more accurate title would be Nuance Is A Sleeping Pill.
Whatever.

My point is still the same.

And that point is, when it comes to communicating a political idea in today's environment, less is more. And exploring all of the facets, possible exceptions, anomalies, considerations, caveats, counter-examples, logic, counter-logic, amendments, provisos, clauses, riders, and so on, muddies comprehension and kills enthusiasm, if it doesn't gut the message of all vitality and coherence.

Compare these ...

Version 1:

A strong case can be made that while on occasion defense department funding finds its way into both the public schools and university level institutions — usually in the form of research grants — the extreme weight given to military spending by the federal government has created shortages of essentials required by our public schools.

Version 2:

Bombs or books. It's our choice.

They say the same thing. Yes, the first sounds more articulate, erudite. But the second one in six words says what needs to be said to a voter. If he or she wants more information and analysis, that is certainly available. In fact, there so much of it available, that often people's heads explode just sampling it. All they really need to key in on, when trying to sort through the sound bites, doublespeak, and frothy mumbo jumbo being served up in the typical election cycle is: *What's the choice here? What do these candidates stand for? What's the difference between them? If I choose Candidate B over Candidate A, what will I be getting?*

People are busy. They don't have time to read books, political analysis, the pros and cons — written by pros and *cons* — they typically don't have time to pore over campaign literature and read position papers posted on websites, professional and academic journals. They might catch a TV spot, or listen to what a candidate says in a news channel interview. Sadly, these highly scripted and choreographed public appearances often feature what we see above in Version 1. Often a candidate will "nuance" and qualify everything so thoroughly, it's next to impossible for anyone to figure out what's being said, or what promises are being made. This is, of course, very intentional. Often a candidate doesn't want voters to know where he or she actually comes down on specific issues.

This is entirely the opposite of what we should be demanding. It is just this sort of verbal gymnastics and sleight of mouth which has poisoned electoral politics. Candidates at the federal and state level have teams of psychologists, media experts, image consultants, and election politics professionals, to fashion an appealing but often ambiguous, even vaporous campaign message.

We deserve some straight talk.

Actually, we more than deserve it. We should insist on it.

Predictably, on the rare occasions they get it …

Voters find it refreshing!

It's a welcome change from the tedium of empty rhetoric, garrulous showboating, and disingenuous posturing.

Is Version 2 simplistic? Or is it just straightforward?

Remember, this sort of simple, direct, easy-to-grasp language parallels and is supported by the entire petition/contract strategy.

The petition as prep work for the candidate contract is concise and direct. While the contracts themselves by necessity include a bunch of legalisms, the core commitment to taking action with respect to each designated issue is unambiguous and straightforward.

Thus a GP/I candidate can decisively say: *"I'm for more books and fewer bombs. I will fight for better education. I have made a legally binding commitment. I signed a contract with you, the voters."*

People will understand it.

Voters will know that this is not empty campaign blather.

Straight talk. Simple and clear.

No equivocation. No obfuscation. No excuses. No nonsense.

Minimum wage: *"I will fight to raise the minimum wage to $15/hour. I signed a contract with the voters."*

Ending the wars: *"I will sponsor legislation to end the wars. I signed a contract with the voters."*

GMO labeling: *"I will introduce a bill in Congress and fight for GMO labeling. I signed a contract with the voters."*

Social security: *"I will protect social security. I signed a contract with the voters."*

Medicare: *"I will protect Medicare. I signed a contract with the voters."*

Fair taxation: *"I will go to Congress and fight for increasing the both the upper income tax and capital gains tax rates to at least 60%. I signed a contract with the voters."*

There is no need for, no place for, no excuse for nuance here.

How many times have you heard it?

"Say what you mean and mean what you say."

That's it!
Keep it short.
Keep it sweet.
Make it direct.
Make it clear.

CHAPTER THIRTEEN

Branding

Branding is a good thing for whatever is branded.

Branding is the product of pull or push, ideally both.

Pull branding is when something gains respectability, desirability, etc. and the public begins to automatically identify it as a thing of value. People like a certain soft drink. They tell their friends and neighbors. More people like it. Suddenly, anything with that drink's logo is regarded with glee, embraced with positive associations. People flock to the store and kill themselves with a sweet baptism of their gullets.

Push branding is PR. It's Madison Avenue. It's people running in slow motion through fields with lovely music playing. It's cute kids and adorable old folk full of giggles and delight. It's burly men with beer running off their chins onto their delicious chests while they hang by their fingertips from a mile high vertical shear. It's a seductive woman poured into yoga pants and a revealing halter top gliding across the room spraying air freshener. Viewers of television and other media are trained, conditioned to have warm fuzzies about whatever is being advertised. Sometimes it's not even clear what it is. But it sure seems like you have to have it, *whatever* it is.

Once the branding is successful, whatever the product or idea might be has smooth sailing ahead in terms of "marketing". People buy warm fuzzies. Just because ... they do.

It would be great for a minor political party to achieve fantastic branding. I am, of course, thinking here first and foremost of the Green Party, which already has some visibility on the political landscape. With confidence in the two major parties now plunging, were the Green Party able to achieve a major makeover — a rehabilitation of its current image as a quirky fringe party at best, a dangerous "spoiler" at worst — it would be elegantly positioned to step in and fill the growing vacuum that exists in our volatile political environment. If people felt as good about it as they do about the John Lewis *Monty the Penguin* ad, problem solved. The Green Party could take over the world!

Two critical factors consign this daydream to the hope chest of far flung fantasies, at least for now.

1) There's not enough time. It is a long, daunting uphill battle, to put it mildly.

2) Third-parties, particularly the Green and Socialist parties, have already been branded, negatively smeared beyond immediate redemption. It's a sad, ugly truth.

How this reality escapes GP political strategists is beyond me.

I cannot emphasize this too strongly.

If a candidate wants to be taken seriously, he or she MUST downplay their running on a minor-party ticket.

I don't mean hide it.

I am not proposing deception.

I am merely insisting on facing the hard facts and dealing with them realistically.

Anyone who makes a speech or has a photo op beneath a banner which says 'Green Party' or 'Socialist Party' or even 'Libertarian Party' — which actually has more registered voters than the Green Party — has just signed a death warrant for their campaign. Ears slam shut. Eyes avert. People immediately start making excuses why they CANNOT vote for this person.

Pull branding is out of the question. There are just far too few success stories and despite the best efforts of some very brilliant, energetic people, 99.99% of the public doesn't know and doesn't care about them. There has to be a lot of word-of-mouth, an enormous amount of buzz, over a very long period of time, for pull branding to rise above the chaotic and cacophonous din of the media jungle, and to become a coherent and forceful presence.

How it happens is often as mysterious as why it happens. Some product or icon will capture the imagination of the public and explode on the scene as a new meme or hot new brand. It typically doesn't happen with politicos, unless they do something exceptionally scandalous or deliciously obscene. Usually that's not the kind of branding we're looking for anyway.

Push branding requires enormous amounts of money. It happens in politics, for sure. The whole Tea Party phenomenon would have died on the vine and enjoyed minor cult status if it weren't for the infusion of cash and covert takeover by the Koch brothers.

The point I'm trying to make here is this.

While "building a viable third party" is a noble and necessary endeavor, there is not enough time for any minor party to gain sufficient respectability, believability or electability to win the coming elections *as a party*.

You might hear people say, "I'm voting for the Democrat."

You might hear people say, "I'm voting for the Republican."

But with a rarity that makes winning the lottery look practically like a certainty, will you ever hear, "I'm voting for the Green."

I'm not talking syntactical inconsistency or even cognitive disjunction.

I'm talking political reality.

The next election represents a crossroads and opportunity of historic proportion.

If the Republican-Democratic corporate duopoly is not soon overthrown, it will be game over for possibly decades to come.

At the same time, recognize that public distrust and dissatisfaction with the state of our politics, is at a historical high. Not since the late 19th Century has there been so much obvious discontent and disconnect between the voting public and the professional class of politicos.

People are looking to make a change.

However, I don't see them wanting to change parties.

I see them wanting to change the *people* elected to office.

If instead of worrying about building party loyalty and the refurbishing the brand of a minor party, we give the voting public district-by-district a *real live human being* to swap out their current legislators with, I think there is a real chance.

I will repeat this message as many ways as I can, because I think it's so crucial.

There's no time to educate the public about what in their eyes will appear to be a new, "upstart" party. For example, there's no time for the Green Party to overcome the "spoiler" stigma, the "tree-hugger" label, or any of the other malignant misunderstanding that plagues them, and then get people to appreciate what an amazing and wonderful vision they have laid out for America in their party platform.

But taking it district-by-district as a *personal* contest: 'Your incumbent has promised this. But he votes against it time and time again. This guy/gal here understands what you want. He/she has signed a legal contract, which neither the Democrat or Republican will sign. He/she is under legal obligation to go to Washington DC to get the job done right!'

That will produce some immediate results.

If voters feel passionate about a particular issue and two, three, four others like it, they just may come around and break their major party habit. They might just give this new guy/gal a shot, because they're fed up with never getting results. They won't care whether he/she is Green or Bull Elk, Populist, Sons of Houdini, Hells Angels, or Friends of Justin Bieber.

• • •

Speaking of branding, let's up the ante here a bit and talk about the presidential election.

What candidate represents the most powerful, prominent, towering, unavoidable *brand* in the upcoming contest for magisterial ruler of the United States of America and the world, aka POTUS?

(If you get this wrong, you will be stripped of your diplomas, driving license, credit cards, and citizenship!)

Yes ... Hillary Clinton.

And what is the Hillary brand? What does it represent?

First, let me say that the Hillary brand is a powerful combination of both push and pull branding. She throws around a lot of iconic and legendary weight purely having been first lady of Wild Bill Clinton, then Senator Hillary Clinton, capped off with Secretary of State Hillary Clinton.

But along the way there has been a lot of the best image-making money could buy, which continues to this day, revved up now to awe-inspiring RPMs of spin. Some of the push branding is damage control for the pull branding, the accumulation of bad posturing, overt self-aggrandizement, general pushiness, and some grotesque policy choices. Supporting the Iraq war is the first of many that comes to mind, which naturally after a massage by the spin doctors comes out as "this lady is tough".

Right. No one is going to push Hillary around. Look at the hundreds of thousands of bodies we piled up in Iraq, Afghanistan, Libya. There's your proof!

A big push is now underway to fashion this warmongering lapdog for the military-industrial complex, this groveling sycophant to the corporate oligarchy, this *very wealthy* card-carrying member of the 1%, as a candidate of the people. Aah yes, that sweet lady next door who you can borrow a cup of sugar from. More like the steely woman whose lawyer your lawyer can contact to recapitalize some credit default swaps.

We'll see how the reinvented "populist Hillary" plays out under the artillery fire of what's left of progressive voices in the media. Never underestimate, however, the power of well-crafted PR or the gullibility of the American public.

But all of that is really sub-text.

Because what is the *meme*, the high concept burble, the *towering babble of conceit* which constitutes about 99.99999% of the Hillary brand?

(If you get *this* wrong, we might have to BEHEAD YOU!)

Ready? ...

First female president in the history of the United States of America!
Unbelievable!

People are looking at this as some sort of historical inevitability.

She and she alone is the embodiment of *destiny!*

There are 165,000,000 females in our country. And Hillary is the *only one* qualified, the one female knighted by the provident crowned head of fate, the one female chosen by history.

People are buying this!

Talk about the power of branding.

But let me point out what should be obvious.

The *first female president in history* meme has a vulnerability as big as the Hindenburg.

There *are* 165,000,000 females in America.

And if there *were* another viable female candidate? ...

Hmm! Let's think about this.

Thinking ... thinking ...

She's got to be bright, progressive, articulate, shovel-ready, an experienced campaigner.

Thinking ... thinking ...

Oh! Got it! The one *I voted for* last presidential election.

Jill Stein!

There goes the Hillary brand, folks! Poof! In one awe-inspiring deflation of the Hillary brand blimp.

Dr. Jill Stein is brilliant, courageous, strong — can't have some woman who just wants to vacuum the White House and bake cookies to send to Kim Jong-un — not a corporate lap dancer for Wall Street and the rest of the oligarchs. And Jill Stein has something completely lacking in Hillary Clinton: integrity. Therefore, she will not spend half of her campaign defending against scandals, secret alliances, hidden agendas.

She's the real thing!

Did I mention, she's a *female?*

The one big problem — and Dr. Stein, I apologize for my bluntness, if you happen to be reading this — is so few people know who she is, Kathy Wolf of the Home Shopping Network has better name recognition.

Yes, I'm serious.

I wish I had $20 for every time when I tell people who I voted for in the last election I get, "Who is Jill Stein?"

This is not to discredit or criticize anything Dr. Stein or her dedicated campaign staff, or the Green Party itself, has done to promote her presidential aspirations.

It is an indictment of a process that systematically locks out alternative voices, ruthlessly crushes minor-party participation, aggressively tips the scales to exclude a meaningful, *democratic* challenge to the plutocracy underwritten by the two-party charade we must now endure under the cruelly ironic misnomer, *American democracy*. There is nothing American — at least in terms of the values we claim as Americans to hold dear — or democratic about the current electoral system.

Dr. Jill Stein has been marginalized. The Green Party has been demonized.

It is the spoiler party. It is the loser party.

There is no avoiding this fact. This is reality. Anyone running against the Democrats and Republicans must accept that their minor party status is a liability of biblical proportions. Intentionally and fiendishly, the two major parties, with the full complicity of main stream media, have been hugely successful at lumping minor parties in with lepers, child molesters, traitors, and the clinically insane.

Under these insidious conditions, how is it possible for a minor-party candidate to get elected to the highest office of the land?

The same principle applies to a presidential candidate as a candidate at any level.

Assuming we can get the word out — and we can (see Chapter Ten: *Getting the Word Out* and Chapter Eleven: *Messaging* — while acknowledging that task in itself is a formidable challenge, let me again emphasize one of the most important concepts I am arguing here, in stark and straightforward terms ...

The public will vote for an *individual,* minor party or independent, who can *guarantee* them something they *really truly desperately* want, which neither major party candidate can deliver.

It's that simple.

Go back to 1992 and the Ross Perot campaign. From Wikipedia ...

> Spawned by the American dissatisfaction with the political system, grassroots organizations sprang up in every state to help Perot achieve ballot access . . . Perot focused the campaign on his plans to balance the federal budget, further economic nationalism, strengthen the war on drugs and implement "electronic town halls" throughout the nation for direct democracy.

Granted, times were different.

'Balance the federal budget'? Scratch that.

'Strengthen the war on drugs'? Forget about it.

'Further economic nationalism'? Hmm.

'Implement electronic town halls'? That's still a winner now.

'Direct democracy'? Rather than corrupt non-representation? Yes!

'American dissatisfaction with the political system'? Exactly! Maybe even more so now.

Ross Perot mostly funded his own campaign. But I remember those days well. He had a huge, fanatical following of volunteers, people who were almost as obnoxious as he was, drubbing everyone within earshot. They were crazed!

Talk about a less-than-ideal presidential candidate. The guy was an eyesore, a snarky little weasel who sounded like a carnival barker or a second-string rodeo announcer.

And he was a self-sabotaging idiot. He even quit the race midway in a childish tantrum.

He reentered October 1, in time to participate in the debates.

He still ended up getting 18.91% of the popular vote.

I hardly suggest his campaign "strategy" — if you want to abuse the term that badly — as a model for a serious attempt at the White House these days. Times are *very different* now.

I bring this up for only one reason.

The lesson to take away is just what I said earlier.

A substantial number of voters thought Perot could deliver something they didn't think they would get from the two major party candidates. Even in hindsight, it's hard for me to quite figure out what that was.

But there's no way to look down our noses at 18.91% of the popular vote. He was saying something and somebody was listening.

18.91%!

It is possible. We saw it happen.

Of course, the barricades are higher and more daunting these days.

It's almost impossible to get a minor party candidate the opportunity to participate in a campaign debate, certainly not the glamour parade of the presidential debates.

On the other hand, more than ever the 24/7/365 news tapeworm has a bigger appetite than ever. The writhing news machine is a big, bloated beast that eats anything, as long as it smacks of controversy and promises a lot of bloodshed, real or figurative.

Sad to have to put it so bluntly, so cynically.

But it offers hope. Dangle a chunk of newsworthy meat before the slobbering jaws of CNN, Fox, MSNBC and just be careful you don't get your head bitten off!

• • •

How about this?

I say there is something which is so rarely seen in the media, so unique and shockingly powerful, it is guaranteed by it's very essence to shake the foundations of contemporary society and get the media talking puppets alternating between fits of hyperventilating euphoria and reeling histrionics.

Do you want to know what that is?

This one rare apocalyptic thing?

Get ready. This is no joke.

It's ... the TRUTH.

Packaged properly, of course ...

It'll take the world by storm!

Why?

Because the *truth* about our economy, our democracy, the plutocratic overthrow of our potentially amazing system of government, the *truth* about the endless wars for profit, the looting of our economy and our treasury by the rich, the shadow government, the *truth* about the rogue and destructive role of the CIA in world affairs, the overreach of the NSA and other security agencies, the militarization of the police, all of this and more, ARE BLOODY, HORRIBLE SCANDALS!

It would be hard to make up a more horrifying story which sums up the current state of our nation and the self-sabotaging direction we are headed.

I say this as someone who writes novels!

It's difficult to come up with fiction as extreme and aberrant as the reality we are living in.

Get the TRUTH out there and believe me … it'll go viral!

Even without the support of the mainstream media.

At the same time, we can count on one thing.

MSM will eventually come around.

If any of this stuff starts to get critical mass, all of it *will* be headlined day-after-day by the mainstream media. They eat it up like the insatiable busybodies they have become.

They could never pass up scandal and drama like this.

It's too good for their advertising budgets.

CHAPTER FOURTEEN

The Honor System

I used to have a small office. Six employees.

We used a snack service where twice a week a small snack dispenser would be delivered and plopped down next to our Mr. Coffee drip machine. It was a cardboard affair. Fold the top back and there arrayed for our junk food cravings were bags of peanuts, chips, pretzels, crackers, cookies, a wide variety of candy bars and other typical under-a-dollar snacks. In one corner was attached a small square money box, also just cardboard, with a slot on top for us to insert payment. We got to know the bloke that delivered our nutritionless but pleasing treats — this was his own little business enterprise — and would never consider short-changing him.

Back in those days, people as a general rule were quite honest, and thus a lot of things operated on the honor system. It was considered bad form and unconscionable to cheat on arrangement like this.

Elections are based on the honor system.

It has been that way since the birth of our nation.

A candidate tells the voters what he or she will do for them. They vote for candidates based on their "word" to deliver on their promises.

Why then replace such an entrenched time-honored system based on trust, with one which introduces legal instruments — aka candidate contracts — which enforceably bind our elected officials to their constituents to specific terms of service?

Is it because we have an uneasy feeling?

Is it because we have a sneaking suspicion?

Is it because we have some ill-defined misgivings?

Is it because we have an inkling that something's not right?

Nope. None of the above.

No uneasy feeling, suspicion, nebulous misgivings, no inkling.

On the contrary.

It's because we now know with <u>absolute</u> <u>certainty</u> …

OUR POLITICIANS CAN'T BE TRUSTED!

The record is crystal clear.

Every election cycle it's the same. The baby-kissing, the lofty speeches, the backslapping, the glad-handing, the photo ops, the teary-eyed anecdotes.

Bumper stickers! Yard signs! More good paying jobs! A strong economy!

And despite soothing reassurances — even explicit promises and clear commitments — on every single important front, things continue to deteriorate. We might win a small victory here and there. But we continue to lose the war.

The honor system.

That portable box of snacks could never work in today's political environment. Sure, some decent congressmen would ante up their quarters for a bag of chips or a Snickers bar. But others wouldn't pay at all. Still others would cut open the little payment box and steal the money. Some would take campaign contributions from XYZ Foods International to insist that the box be removed and replaced by a steel-reinforced vending machine. A couple would have the vendor investigated and charged under the Espionage Act because he put free copies of one of Kahlil Gibran's poems next to the tiny bags of red licorice.

The honor system only works with honorable people.

Look around you.

Would you trust any of our current crop of politicos with your house keys?

The candidate contracts introduce a level of certainty never seen before in our history.

At least on the specific issues addressed in the contracts, we *know* how our elected representatives will perform.

That certainty can mean a big difference in a time awash with unreliability and prevarication.

Thus, it's time for a dramatic change.

A paradigm shift.

No more honor system.

On key issues, the ones that have the great support of the American people but are opposed by the plutocrats and corporate toadies now in office, we *will* demand a legally binding commitment in writing.

The American people have told their representatives how to vote. The representatives didn't listen.

Now we will *require* them to comply with our demands. We will put it in writing and force them to sign it. No signature. No vote. No cushy job in Washington DC.

The time for candidate contracts is now.

What's the alternative?

Continued dysfunction and treachery?

Complete tyranny?

CHAPTER FIFTEEN

Contracts

One last comment about the candidate contract …

Don't even try to tell me that America doesn't get warm and giggly about 'contracts'.

Yes, the phrase 'Candidate Contracts' sounds solemn, legalistic, formal.

Do you remember Newt Gingrich's *Contract With America*?

Granted, it was a fluffy, pointless piece of right wing propaganda.

But people loved it!

It sounded so bold and decisive, so *official*.

A contract with the people of America to set things right.

If Americans could cheer that hollow piece of hot air, they surely will get behind a set of legitimate contracts which in fact *will* get America on track.

They will celebrate a new era where politicians actually do what they're told to do.

They will take great satisfaction in finally having their voices heard.

They will take pride in a system that at least starts to look like …

Government of the people, by the people, for the people!

PART II:

Because I never underestimate the power of muddled thinking and pessimism to kill good ideas, I've saved the best for last.

The only flaw in what follows is that it *could* work.

Now *that's* scary.

What? No more whining? No more excuses? No more blaming the Republicans?

What I am about to describe represents such a powerful tool for winning the next crucial election, and boasts qualities rarely seen in the tragicomic gyrations of our current politicos — honesty and boldness are two that immediately come to mind — those who choose to oppose it do so because it risks shaking the very foundations of our system, not as configured, but as it is now implemented. Business as usual will come to an end, hence a lot of these poor folks will end up out of work. I hardly feel any sympathy. They are the ones who should be out of work. They are the pathetic miscreants who will be replaced by the more competent, visionary, ethical, and just plain sensible individuals who have been shut out of politics for too long.

$$\bullet \bullet \bullet$$

I am not anti-government.

In fact, as a left-of-left liberal, as a radical progressive, as a neo-Marxist, I am *for* big government.

I am for big government — democratically guided and responsibly controlled by the citizens of our country — which is sensitive to the needs of the people, one which aggressively and efficiently pursues every possible appropriate initiative in the public interest, one which promotes the overall welfare of the public and fosters prosperous and fulfilling lives for all of our citizens.

Having said that, I concede there is a ton of waste in government.

To some degree, this is a product of scale, and is unavoidable.

To a some degree, the waste has to do with inefficiencies and bad management.

But to a greater degree, the waste is a product of misplaced priorities and bad policy decisions.

I'm not interested at this time in exploring remedies along these lines to this enormous challenge.

Not directly anyway.

What I *am interested in*, however, is <u>exploiting</u> the appalling waste to enormous political advantage.

In particular, I am focusing here on profligate spending by the military establishment, and all of the waste which results from the ongoing promotion of aggression and war.

Whether the public is very aware or genuinely concerned about it, there are astronomical amounts of their tax dollars being thrown away on defense, war, and related activities.

It's time they started paying attention.

It's time they start getting mad.

It's time to use this enormous powder keg of potential outrage for regime change.

CHAPTER SIXTEEN

The Speech

I will now present the *Peace Dividend* strategy as it would be announced to the public in the form of a speech by a GP/I candidate for high office — the Senate, House of Representatives, or for the presidency.

> *What I'm about to tell you will make you very angry. Though it is entirely true — yes, I can prove beyond any shadow of a doubt every single assertion I am about to make — you will not hear this from any but a handful of candidates running for office, certainly not from any Democrat or Republican, since they are responsible for everything I am about to describe.*
>
> *Here we go.*
>
> *Every person with me here today, plus almost 180 million other good, decent, patriotic Americans who have paid their taxes in good faith for the last 24 years, have been ripped off. Folks, we have been the victims of the biggest theft in human history.*
>
> *Let me explain.*
>
> *Back in 1992 right after the collapse of the Soviet Union, we were promised something called the "peace dividend". Our adversary for over four decades was gone, the Cold War was over. We could breathe easy now, start diverting all the money we had spent in the weapons race with the USSR on other things, education, infrastructure, investments in peaceful technology.*
>
> *Well, it never happened. In fact, over the course of the last 24 years, the defense budget has increased 16 times! It really took off in the last decade-and-a-half. This year it is more than double what it was in 2000.*
>
> *Mind you, this is the "official" budget for the Department of Defense.*

There are all sorts of defense expenditures and top secret programs that are tucked inside other departmental budgets, or off-budget entirely. This year over $12 billion is hidden in the Department of Energy budget for nuclear weapons. More than $50 billion goes for what's termed the "black budget" of the NSA. Billions and billions go into 1,271 government organizations and 1,931 private companies working on counterterrorism programs, homeland security and intelligence, allegedly making us safer. You have to wonder if ISIS is getting a good laugh out of that? The safer we get, the more territory they take over and the more people they behead.

Think about this. While our bridges and roads are falling apart, the U.S. government paid out $150 billion — yes, 150 billion of your tax dollars — to rebuild Iraq and Afghanistan. Not $150 billion to repair our schools, build some parks and recreation centers for our children to play in. Not funding for libraries or day care, nutrition programs. No, America spent $150 billion to rebuild two countries we didn't have to destroy in the first place.

And speaking of the wars in Afghanistan and Iraq, just look at this chart.

US War Spending Since 9/11

How taxpayer dollars were spent on Iraq, Afghanistan, and other war-related activities

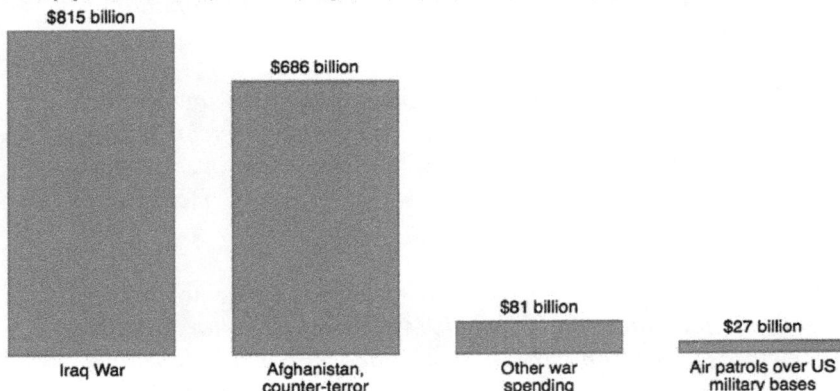

$815 billion	$686 billion	$81 billion	$27 billion
Iraq War	Afghanistan, counter-terror	Other war spending	Air patrols over US military bases

Source: Congressional Research Service

Mind you, we didn't have to fight either the war in Afghanistan or Iraq. There were no weapons of mass destruction in Iraq. We didn't have to go after Osama bin Laden in Afghanistan. The Taliban government offered to hand him over, as long as we wouldn't bomb their country. So we bombed it.

These two wars which so far have cost us $1.5 trillion dollars — and experts have estimated will end up costing us $4 to $5 trillion — were a complete fraud.

This insane squandering of lives and money on unnecessary wars obviously should and must stop.

You and I must make it stop.

Work with me and we can make it stop!

But that is only one half of the equation. Yes, stopping this will save us making the same mistakes in the future. But what about the $1.5 trillion already gone up in smoke? This is your money. This is my money. We worked hard and sacrificed. We paid our taxes in good faith, believing the lies we were told. We were deceived into turning over our hard-earned dollars, money we could have used right here in America for our families and communities.

I say there is only one way to address this appalling injustice.

I say there is only one proper and responsible way to make up to the American people the enormous financial losses they have endured — the gross misuse of taxpayer money in the two wars and gross squandering of money on completely unnecessary military programs.

I've put together a list — a summary of the ways our arrogant politicians have thrown our tax dollars to the wind on war and the military. Bear in mind these are conservative estimates. We are still studying this and these figures may even be adjusted upwards. But as it stands now, here's what it looks like:

War Reparations Payable
To American Taxpayers

EXCESSIVE BASIC D.O.D. SPENDING: 1992 - 2015	$2,504,000,000,000
AFGHANISTAN WAR: 2001 - 2015	686,000,000,000
IRAQ WAR: 2003 - 2015	815,000,000,000
OTHER WARS: 2001 - 2015	81,000,000,000
AIR PATROL PROTECTION U.S. BASES: 2001 - 2015	27,000,000,000
EXCESSIVE N.S.A. BLACK BUDGETING: 2001 - 2015	260,000,000,000
UNNECESSARY D.H.S. SPENDING: 2003 - 2015	151,000,000,000
TOTAL DUE:	**$4,524,000,000,000**

Like I said, this is probably on the low end, but at bare minimum over the past 24 years, the wars, the insane military build-up, our building over 900 bases in 136 countries, the funding of boondoggles like the F-35, conservatively has squandered $4.52 trillion of our tax money.

That's TRILLION! I repeat, for those of you who may be in shock, $4.52 trillion!

Now, let's say you buy a fruit blender or a hair drier from a store, and when you take it home you find out it doesn't work. What do you do? You return to the store, then either get a replacement or you get your money back.

113

Unfortunately, there's no way to get a replacement with the horrifying waste on my list. Even more tragically, we can't bring back to life the brave men and women whose lives were lost. We can't turn the clock back.

But what we can do is get our money back.

And that, my fellow Americans, is exactly what I'm proposing.

We're going to get back all of this money. It's our money. We paid it to our government in taxes. We expected them to do the right things with it. We trusted them. And they lied to us.

However, we didn't just get a defective fruit blender or broken hair drier. We got defective wars, defective military equipment, defective leadership. We got a defective economy where only the rich do well and for the rest of us it's broken. Since they wasted trillions of dollars, now we have broken bridges, broken roads, broken schools, broken communities. We have bankruptcies and foreclosures. Enough!

We want our money back.

We will demand our money back.

This $4.52 trillion is owed to the American people!

Now, notice the title of my invoice: War Reparations Payable To American Taxpayers.

Why do I call them war reparations? Because most of this outrageous balance due is a result of two major wars that we were lied into, that never should have been fought, that you and I paid for. And the rest is for the war our elected officials have been conducting on the truth. And us personally! The wars on our families, our schools, the war on each of us, the pillage of taking our hard-earned money under false pretenses, then throwing it down the drain.

I know no other way to put this: This is <u>our</u> money. This is money we could have used. If we Americans had had the $4.52 trillion, we wouldn't be so far in debt, we wouldn't be struggling, our economy wouldn't be stumbling. We would have put it to good use.

We now deserve to have it back, so that belatedly, we <u>can</u> put it to good use. To improve our homes, clothe, feed and educate our kids properly, pay off some of our debts.

We've run the numbers and it comes down to this. Each and every living person who has paid taxes over the past 24 years deserves a refund of $25,416.

You heard that right. Take the $4.52 trillion and divide it by the number of people who in good faith paid taxes over the past 24 years, and that's what you come up with.

So here's what I'm proposing: If I am elected to office, I will fight with every bone in my body to pass legislation, which stipulates that by the end of three calendar years, every living person whose name has appeared on a tax return as a single or joint filer, will receive from the U.S. Treasure a refund of $25,416.

This will be done in three equal installments, starting my first year in office.

If you filed by yourself, you get a payment by the end of next year for $8,472, then two more in the same amount, the two following calendar years. A total refund to each taxpayer of $25,416. If you filed jointly with your husband or wife, <u>each of you</u> gets three identical payments totaling $25,416. As long as you paid taxes, you get a payment.

$8,472 each year for three years in a row.

I call it the Peace Dividend.

Remember? The one promised back in 1992.

Well, I'll finally intend to make good on that promise.

Of course, the Democrats and Republicans who perpetrated this heist are going to scream bloody murder. They're going to say, 'This is outrageous! How can you propose a giveaway of the government's money?'

In the first place, we are a government of the people, by the people, for the people, so it's our money. Second, it's not a giveaway. It's a give-back. Giveaways are what these double-talking politicians do when they give tax breaks to their rich friends and corporate subsidies to companies like GE and Exxon, who are already up to their eyebrows in cash. This is a refund for defective services. This is a refund for a broken America that we paid for.

Then of course they're going to scream, 'How can we afford it? You'll bankrupt the country!' Gee, it's funny how when we need to protect oil and gas industry interests by attacking countries which pose no threat to us, we can find the hundreds of billions of dollars. No problem. Funny how when the big banks are teetering on the brink of bankruptcy, we can instantly find $750 billion to bail them out. And by the way, that was the tip of the iceberg. The Federal Reserve actually bailed them out to the tune of $16 trillion. Yes, you heard that right. $16 trillion. And I didn't get that from some socialist web site. I read about it in Forbes Magazine.

To those who say we can't afford it, let me give you some advice. Don't insult the intelligence of the American people. Moreover, don't question the power of American ingenuity. We'll find the money. We have already completed a comprehensive plan and can come up with the $4.52 trillion, and more if necessary. We can do it in ways that are good for the American people — all of the American people, not just the ones who belong to country clubs — good for the American economy, good for the future of our children.

I will present in the near future the details of the entire plan. But let me give you a little hint by talking about an appalling reality that is undermining our democracy and destroying the American Dream.

Wealth inequality is at an all-time high. How did this happen? That's easy. The money went from your pockets as tax-payers into the bank accounts of the wealthy. They're the ones who make money on war, on military spending. They're the ones who rake in huge profits, while our fine young men and women die in senseless wars that just make more enemies and create more wars. They are also the ones on the receiving end of the bank bailouts, the tax breaks, the oil industry and pharmaceutical industry subsidies. They are the ones who get tax incentives for hiding their money offshore and shipping our jobs overseas.

This all has got to stop. This is going to stop. You're going to make it stop.

If I'm elected and a sufficient number of others like me get elected — so that our democracy is finally back in the hands of you, the people — we're going to put an end to this reverse Robin Hood con job once and for all. No more robbing the poor to give to the rich. No more lying to the American public. No more buying elections. No more profit over people.

We'll start with the Peace Dividend of $25,416 and go from there. We'll start making America work again for everyone, not just the elite ultra-wealthy.

• • •

The candidate contract for the *Peace Dividend* will read as follows:

I, *[Name of Candidate]*, if elected to a seat in the U.S. House of Representatives, hereby commit to co-sponsor and vote in favor of legislation which instructs the U.S. Treasury to remit payment totaling $25,416 to every living American citizen who has filed a tax return since 1992, payment to be made in three equal installments of $8,472 each. Disbursement shall take place in three consecutive calendar years, beginning the first year of my term in office. This total remittance of $25,416 shall apply in whole to what is referred to as the *Peace Dividend*, an amount not less than $4.52 trillion due and payable to tax payers in the form of a refund, satisfying a debt obligation incurred

117

between 1992 and 2015, as a result of collecting tax revenue under false pretenses, and/or misuse and misallocation of those revenues.

I will not resist, discourage, or in any manner put up an impediment to, and in fact will publicly and on the floor of Congress actively promote, any and all legislation in support of this measure. If no other legislator comes forth to offer such legislation, I will create and introduce by my own initiative, within 90 days of taking office, such a legislative act for consideration by Congress.

I further understand and fully agree to the following: If I violate the above-stated terms of this pledge, I will tender on the 91st day after taking the oath of office for my legislative seat, my full and unqualified resignation from this elected position. Moreover, within one year of my resignation, I will refund all contributions made by individual donors in support of my candidacy for this office.

This entire pledge constitutes a legally binding contract between myself and that class of citizens who will be my constituents, should I win the upcoming election. In the event that I fail to perform the above-required actions, redress may be sought by those same citizens in the form of a class-action suit in a civil court of law, and I will be liable for a minimum of $10,000,000 damages for breach of contract. If I fail to resign from office due to my failure to fulfill the other requirements of this contract or related contracts, I may be liable for an additional class-action settlement for an amount not less than $50,000,000. No portion of these specified settlements may be paid from campaign donations, PACs or SuperPACs.

I take this pledge voluntarily and with full appreciation of my responsibility to the citizens of the *[Name of Congressional District]* should they choose me as their elected representative. I accept the terms of this pledge as legally binding, and with a thorough and lucid understanding of its requirements and consequences.

Signed: _____

Date: _____

This formulation is for an individual running for the House of Representatives, but it is just as applicable and can be configured for Senate races, even for the presidency.

CHAPTER SEVENTEEN

Selling the Peace Dividend

At first selling the idea to the voting public will be an uphill battle.

But not for long.

The middle class will initially be somewhat wary. Many will say: *"I don't know if this candidate is right or not, but it sure would work out nicely if he or she is. I need to hear more."*

We will have gotten their ear.

AT LEAST THEY'LL BE PAYING ATTENTION!

That was the goal in the first place, eh? Getting people to notice and listen to minor-party candidates, take them seriously for a change.

If the groundwork is properly in place using petitions and candidate contracts on other critical issues, this audacious and radical proposal will at least be taken seriously, even though not universally embraced.

As the rationale behind the Peace Dividend is explained over and over, it will begin to sink in. The idea of receiving a substantial sum of money for any reason will lubricate the mental machinery. For some reason, people like getting money. They will listen and be thinking. Gradually steady progress will occur. They will *want* to believe what they hear is true. It's just a matter of making a sincere and sensible case, breaking through previous brainwashing and the expected storm of criticism by the puppet media. Our tap tap tapping away at the artifice, the wall of disinformation, offering a believable narrative, must be consistent and relentless.

The middle class will eventually come around.

The poor and economically troubled will embrace the plan right away. They have been screwed for so long by "the man", they will have no trouble believing that they have been lied to and ripped off. The possibility that the tide is being turned and for once some of Uncle Sam's stash is coming their way will be much needed and dearly welcome relief. The poor in this country have been ravaged disproportionately by the wars and the moral bankruptcy of our skewed national priorities. They know it. They live the results of this gross injustice every day.

The crucial challenge is *getting these poor folks to vote*. That there is a vast pool of dispirited people who have given up on the system and don't vote goes without saying. The prospect of getting a windfall through the *Peace Dividend* should be a powerful incentive, but it will still require some organizational effort — voter registration and physical transportation to the polls.

• • •

Understandably, there will be a firestorm from the Democrats and Republicans, the corporate media, the sycophants who like dogs sniff the crotches of the plutocrats at every opportunity. Think tanks and academic puppets will go on the attack.

This is actually all very good.

As I said before and will say repeatedly …

You can't buy advertising like this. It's free!

Every attack is an opportunity to make our case.

If that sounds daunting, please remember that in some ways this is a very easy sell.

The lies about the Afghanistan and Iraq wars are increasingly becoming common knowledge.

There is so much waste in the military, so many boondoggle projects, so much pork, it's difficult to know where to start.

Fire away …

The DOD purchased $16 billion worth of ammunition that it didn't actually need, then spent $1 billion destroying it.

The $1.5 trillion F-35 can't fly in the rain and has been grounded for engine failure. It has been deemed by defense analysts as the biggest major weapons failure initiative in human history.

$500 million worth of U.S. weapons "disappeared" in Yemen.

$300 million "disappears" annually in Afghanistan. Pallets of bundled U.S. currency has been photographed being unloaded from military planes in Kabul.

A $10 billion sea-based X-band radar system was recently scrapped because it didn't work.

The Pentagon itself even admits it has no way to account for $8.5 trillion allocated since 1996! It is suspected much of it went up in smoke.

Finding outrageous examples of DOD waste is almost too easy.

The public should be and will be appalled.

• • •

There will be the usual War On Terror scare tactics.

They are built around entirely bogus but viscerally rousing fear-mongering.

We should be visceral back.

> *"There are horrible terrorist attacks going on in this country. There's no doubt about it. And we should be VERY AFRAID!"*

Then show videos of the police killing innocent, unarmed citizens.

Follow that with video clips of troops and military equipment rolling across vast expanses.

Point out this last video is actually taped in Texas, New Mexico, Arizona, Utah, and southern California, where Jade Helm 15 is being staged. It's the military preparing for war on Americans!

How about a video showing quick clips of military equipment being manufactured?

> *"Yes, America is the #1 arms and military equipment manufacturer in the world, putting out advanced weaponry to keep America safe. Where do these weapons of war end up?"*

Then show clips of ISIS rolling across vast expanses of the Middle East, beheading people. Show the bombing of Yemen by Saudi Arabia, then one of their public beheadings.

"There, ladies and gentlemen, is our wonderful military equipment!"

It's time to be brutally frank with the public.

There's every reason to be both frank and assertive.

We are as a nation headed down an ugly self-destructive path.

What is the reality?

We are arming our own police to attack us.

We are arming the rest of the world to attack us.

That hardly makes us safer.

That makes us the target of more and more aggression.

As Martin Luther King said when he declared he could no longer be silent: "[America is] the greatest purveyor of violence in the world."

People are afraid. They should be.

But they need to be afraid of the correct things.

They need to be afraid of losing an America they can live in, raise their children, have a decent life.

They should be afraid of an America which is being militarized and turned into a police state.

• • •

There will be the obvious accusation that the whole Peace Dividend program is just buying votes.

Here we need to stand very strong.

We must talk about the injustice to the American citizen, the wanton misuse of tax dollars, the systematic draining of money from ordinary citizens for bloated government and completely insane military misadventures. This will definitely appeal to libertarians, even Tea Party nuts. But it will appeal to most everyone as well. People don't like being taken advantage of.

There is some basic, almost crude psychology here. While the Peace Dividend is *exactly* what we claim it is — a refund to the American taxpayer for money collected under false pretenses to prosecute illegal and fraudulent wars — the idea of pennies from Heaven will go a long way to grease the wheels of public acceptance. When people see something in their own best interest, something as astonishing as a windfall of $25,416 coming there way, they will be very willing to look at it in the best possible light. They will *want* to believe it's a good thing. They will be open, even anxious to being persuaded by the logic behind it. They will want the reasons and reasoning to be solid. They will be quietly but enthusiastically hoping it's for real, that it's not some crazy scheme, that getting that much money makes sense and can be justified.

Understandably, at first it will initially seem a little bizarre, off-the-wall. But $25,416 is a nice chunk of change. I think most citizens will be listening *very* carefully, paying very close attention.

The good news is that the supporting evidence *is* real. The plan, as has been demonstrated, *is* solid. This is not a gimmick. This is a wholesome attempt at redressing ugly official malfeasance, of making good on the implicit faith the public puts in its leaders, of making up for losses which resulted from rotten judgment and outright deception of a trusting and credulous citizenry.

Be clear about this.

To redress such theft and abuse, saying sorry is not enough.

A *refund* for broken trust and broken goods is the only satisfactory expression of true regret.

Reparations are compensation for damages. The damage to our economy and society over the past 24 years has been astronomical. The bill has come due.

In spite of the screaming denouncements by the plutocrats, their lapdog politicians and puppet press, I truly believe the general public *will* come around. Honesty and gentle persuasion will go the long mile here.

Any GP/I candidate getting behind this will be heralded as a saint, a national savior, just as FDR was in his day!

President Roosevelt's message was very similar. We have this mess. You good folks didn't cause it. You deserve better. So in the midst of the greatest economic collapse in our history, he established social security for the old folks, unemployment compensation for those who couldn't find work, and created jobs to put 15 million on the public payroll and give them something constructive to do.

Oh my! How the oligarchs and captains of industry screamed back then. But they didn't have a choice. They ended up having to go along with the greatest implementation of "socialist" innovation in our country's history.

Again, we won't give them a choice.

We'll get the people — 300 million plus of them — on our side.

• • •

Let me add this.

I personally don't care how individual citizens work this through in their own minds. I don't care if they have to rationalize it, take it on faith … or even if they consider it a bribe.

It's not a bribe, but people will draw their own conclusions.

I'll tell you why I don't care.

It's the *right thing* to do.

In every respect and to its core, it's an honest attempt to at least *begin* to redress the appalling theft of tax payer money and the callous exploitation of the public trust.

To be entirely candid, it matters not one whit to me if someone says, *"Hell yes, I want my twenty-four thousand bucks. I'll vote for this guy!"*

The intrinsic value of the outcome is not diminished by someone doing the right thing for the wrong reasons.

And as far as I'm concerned, the *Peace Dividend* is only the beginning.

America's riches belong to everyone.

Everybody should get their fair share.

If giving back the $4.52 trillion — that was clearly and undeniably taken under false pretenses from the public and applied to horrible, counter-productive, *destructive* ends — ends up electing good, honest public servants, and situates control of the government rightfully in the hands of the majority of the people, we will have on multiple levels performed a historic public service.

We will have established true representative democracy and saved America from autocratic rule by a tiny elite of self-ordained tyrants.

We will be fulfilling the promise of the Constitution and honoring all those who fought for America's independence from colonial autocracy.

For the first time in a long time, the voice of the people will be heard.

We won't be fretting anymore about the slow migration of the political center ever more to the right.

The political right will get the memorial service it deserves, what is *now the center* will end up being the *extreme right* of the spectrum, and finally a true populist agenda will become the main topic of the national conversation, not some easily-dismissed delusional whining from cranky liberals on the bumbling fringe.

CHAPTER EIGHTEEN

"How will we pay for it?"

How will we pay for it?
Believe it or not, that's the easy part.

1) Peace bonds.
2) Massive tax reform.
3) Financial transaction taxes.
4) Taxing offshore assets and offshored cash.
5) United States Dollars (a peace-based currency for
   domestic use only).

There is one more option but I honestly don't have the necessary understanding of economics to fully appreciate the implications — the pros and cons — of this approach.

6) Minting three $1.5 trillion dollar coins.

Even dismissing for this discussion this last option, it should be acknowledged that the U.S. government is well within its constitutional rights to create such coinage. It's in Article 1: The Legislative Branch, Section 8: Powers of Congress:

> The Congress shall have Power To lay and collect Taxes, Duties, Imposts and Excises, to pay the Debts and provide for the common Defence and general Welfare of the United States; but all Duties, Imposts and Excises shall be uniform throughout the United States; To borrow money on the credit of the United States; To regulate Commerce with foreign Nations, and among the several States, and with the Indian Tribes; To coin Money, regulate the Value thereof …

What I object to right off about this last option is that it undermines fiscal discipline.
That's right. *Fiscal discipline.*
Which is something completely different than fiscal austerity.
A major corollary benefit to the Peace Dividend, one beyond the immediate boost it gives to the consumer economy and redressing the theft

of tax dollars from the American public, is that it *forces* changes of enormous magnitude in our tax laws and tax law enforcement.

When the rich come screaming to the new administration claiming that the Peace Dividend will bankrupt the federal budget, we'll say, "No, it won't. You're going to pay for it." This is exactly what FDR did in the 1930s to stabilize the country, avoid insurrection, and provide much needed relief to millions of desperate Americans.

We're going to slightly reverse things. We're going to provide much needed relief to millions of desperate Americans, essentially making a substantial down payment on attacking the insidious wealth inequality problem with a direct transfer of funds to the 99%, *then* turn to the rich and tell them they need to ante up. We won't be giving them a choice in the matter. The solvency of the country *requires* much greater contributions by them into to U.S. Treasury.

Thus, the Peace Dividend *drives* a whole array of reforms.

For example: boosting the basic income tax over $250,000 to 50%, over $1,000,000 over 60%, on up the income scale. Then, coupling increases in capital gains rates to income tax rates — so the wealthy can't reduce their tax liability the way they do now by transferring their wealth into capital assets — and making similar adjustments to taxing corporations.

It drives reduction and elimination of unnecessary tax breaks and various subsidies.

Perhaps more importantly, it drives a whole new set of laws which attaches responsibility for taxes to offshored accounts and investments. It drives restructuring chartering of corporations and regulation *discouraging* exporting facilities and jobs, imposing huge fines and penalties for moving and basing manufacturing and services overseas, a potential source of substantial revenues for the federal government.

Mint the coins, everything is paid for, and no need exists to raise the money by putting the brakes on the looting of the economy by Wall Street banksters, and the rest of the kleptocracy. Minting the coins pays for the program but doesn't solve systemic problems, which will then come back to haunt us and unravel the overall long term progressive agenda.

I am almost reluctant to point this out, but my approach actually mirrors that of the right wing, and their thus far very successful strategy for undermining the middle class and destroying the social safety net.

The sycophants in Congress blew huge holes in the federal budget with unfunded wars and unconscionable tax breaks for their rich benefactors, then threw up their hands and shrugged, pointed at the burgeoning deficit, and claimed we needed to start *cutting cutting cutting*. With the complicity of our DINO-PINO president, Republicans and sell-out Democrats, then pushed through the sequester, after already attacking a whole host of social programs, education, unemployment compensation, with Social Security and Medicare in the crosshairs as well.

We can play that game too.

We pay the Peace Dividend, throw up our hands and shrug, point to the huge puddle of red ink in the budget, and declare that it's high time to raise some serious money. We'll force the same people who plundered the average American taxpayer by profiting from wars, a bloated military, unnecessary bailouts, and the wanton corrupting of our democracy, to *give back* the money they made at our expense.

They will be forced to pay us back in the form of higher taxes. We'll track down the trillions of dollars of wealth around the world they hide in secret offshore accounts and shadow investments, and force them to ante up their fair share. We'll impose a financial transaction tax to collect an appropriate fee on the "gaming" that goes on in the Wall Street casino. We'll make whatever other reforms are necessary to assure the solvency of the federal government and the robustness of the U.S. economy.

Fiscal discipline is a beautiful thing.

That's what the conservatives have been telling us for years.

• • •

I've already mentioned the essence of what items #2, #3, #4, and #6 entail.

Let me now go into a little detail on items #1 and #5 on my methods for funding the Peace Dividend.

Neither of these — obviously the issuance of bonds but also the creation of special purpose currency — is unprecedented. However, the implementation of each of these under my plan is somewhat original.

• • •

In World War I, the U.S. issued *Liberty Bonds* to raise money for the war. Before World War II, Series E, F and G *U.S. Savings Bonds* were being promoted. Right after the attack on Pearl Harbor, these were sold as *War Bonds*. After that war, the name was switched back.

I remember U.S. Savings Bonds as a kid. They were very popular as birthday and graduation presents and remained so right up until five to ten years ago, when people were no longer inclined or able to save money, therefore stopped buying them.

Never to my knowledge has there been anything called *Peace Bonds* in America.

There should be.

If we can raise money for war, we sure as hell can raise money for peace.

If successful, whatever funds are initially invested in them would go toward covering the Peace Dividend.

People who don't need the entire amount of cash payment for their Peace Dividend could opt to receive all or part of it as *Peace Bonds*, an investment in America's future that would accrue interest and be part of national commitment to focus on peace instead of war in dealing with the rest of the world.

Once the Peace Dividend outlay is covered, *Peace Bonds* could be marketed internationally on the global bond market, inviting other countries to invest in America's peace initiatives, which would include addressing at an international level poverty and health issues, building Third World infrastructure, and whatever other projects would undermine aggression and conflict, and promote harmony in the world.

I don't want to sound like some New Age fruitcake here, but *Peace Bonds* should play a much-needed role in shifting the national consciousness and narrative away from war, perhaps even rehabilitating America's image in the international community as a war-obsessed bully. It seems everything in America now is about the military, war, fighting, bombing, droning. The peace movement is all but dead. Just seeing the word 'peace' *occasionally* might be a refreshing change. It might steer people to thinking about peace as a purposeful and relevant pursuit.

Which brings up item #5, the issuance of special domestic use currency.

• • •

Again, special use currency is not unprecedented.

Abraham Lincoln used "greenbacks", a paper currency backed by nothing more than confidence in the government, to finance the Civil War.

A century later, on June 4, 1963, John F. Kennedy signed Executive Order 11110 which set in motion the issuance of silver certificate notes, currency backed by silver reserves being held at that time by the U.S. Treasury This bypassed the established procedure of borrowing money into circulation from the Federal Reserve. $20 billion of such United States Notes were put in circulation before he was assassinated, many believing it was his introduction of such interest-free debt-free currency which may have prompted his murder.

Risk of assassination aside, no reasonable case can be made against using this power. It is guaranteed by the Constitution. Our current debt-ridden system of going to the private banking institution misleadingly named The Federal Reserve to supply money to the economy is counter-intuitive and in the long term counter-productive.

While ultimately our goal should be to eliminate the Federal Reserve's capacity in this regard, for now we can pick up where Kennedy left off, prudently using what I call *United States Dollars* to cover a sizeable portion of the Peace Dividend remittances.

United States Dollars would look almost exactly like their Federal Reserve Note counterparts. Same layout, same denominations, same founders-of-the-nation images.

Where U.S. currency now says ...

FEDERAL RESERVE NOTE

... *United States Dollars* not surprisingly would say ...

UNITED STATES DOLLARS

Where U.S. currency now says ...

IN GOD WE TRUST

... *United States Dollars* would say ...

PROMOTING PEACE

Where in nearly microscopic print U.S. currency now says ...

THIS NOTE IS LEGAL TENDER
FOR ALL DEBTS, PUBLIC AND PRIVATE

... *United States Dollars* would say ...

THIS NOTE IS LEGAL TENDER FOR ALL DOMESTIC
FINANCIAL TRANSACTIONS, PUBLIC AND PRIVATE

United States Dollars would be for domestic use only. This is to prevent them from being shipped overseas or feeding them into the ongoing currency speculation frenzy. Banks would be instructed to block transfer of *United States Dollars* to non-domestic banking institutions. For example, if a person deposited $8,000 of *United States Dollars* into a domestic account, transfer of funds to non-domestic banks or use of funds for purchases outside the U.S. could only be made from balances in excess of $8,000 accruing from Federal Reserve Note deposits.

This restriction is to guarantee that *United States Dollars* go toward promoting America's domestic economy, i.e. purchasing goods and services "Made in the USA", not exporting any of this newly created wealth, which would only exacerbate our already excessive and out-of-control trade deficit.

Private banks would be encouraged to create *United States Dollars* credit cards. If there is institutional resistance to this by private banks, the U.S. government can fill that need by issuing through its own agencies such credit instruments.

A host of small-business and employee-owned business incentives could be built around *United States Dollars*, for example giving matching federal grants or at least preferential treatment for investing *United States Dollars* in job-creating domestic business start-ups.

If the private bankers don't assassinate our new GP/I president and burn down congressional buildings and office ala the 1933 Reichstag fire, the expansion of general utilization of *United States Dollars* down the road could gradually dismantle the current Debt Doomsday Machine of the Federal Reserve regime.

• • •

Yes, I can hear the outrage now issuing from the solemn faces of the plutocracy.

Part III of this book offers a host of rejoinders to most of the objections we can expect from all those pitiable Wall Street bankers, corporate oligarchs, rich and powerful plunderers who rarely have their positions of privilege and thrones of autocratic rule challenged. Get out the Kleenex. They will cry like spoiled children as they see their control slipping away.

While ideas like candidate contracts, the *Peace Dividend, Peace Bonds,* special purpose domestic currency in the form of *United States Dollars* have not been allowed in the national conversation for many decades, the desperate state of our economy and the dysfunction of our democracy DEMANDS that we start talking about them.

Nothing less than the survival of a recognizable version of America is at stake.

CHAPTER NINETEEN

Necessary Coercion

The oligarchs have been EXTREMELY EFFECTIVE at plundering the economy and stealing the wealth of America from its rightful owners, *all* of the American people.

The method is as simple as it is transparent. But like glass, many don't see it.

The oligarchs start wars, which enrich themselves, then as the federal deficit explodes as a direct consequence of these lucrative misadventures, they throw up their hands and declare, "Oh goodness! We're out of money." They then cut and cancel. Not the programs and initiatives that continue to enrich them — like more military expenditures and anything promoting international instability and subservient puppet states — but everything from food stamps to educational support to health care to the arts — things that spread the wealth around and benefit the vast majority of Americans.

The oligarchs through their reckless but bubble-wealth generating machinations and speculations across the entire spectrum of markets — financial instruments, commodities, capital investment — collapse the system and come "pleading" for help. When massive injections of capital and outright bailouts — which drain the resources of our economy for the rest of us — are complete, they throw up their hands and say, "Oops! There's nothing left now. Sorry! By the way, we sure could use all that money built up in the Social Security Trust. A few trillion dollars would grease the wheels here and there and, you know, get the economy rolling again."

See the pattern? Spend the money, pile up more incomprehensible wealth, then have a panic attack and kill anything which might spread the money around.

What a fraud! What a hoax!

The *Peace Dividend* strategy does *exactly* the same thing but in reverse.

That is, it reverses the flow of wealth upward and starts to direct it where it should go, to its rightful recipients, *all* of the citizens.

We spend the money, i.e. we commit $4.52 trillion to tax payer refunds for prior malfeasance and fraudulent use of tax payer money, then throw up our hands and say, "Golly gee! We have a little problem here. We did the right thing. But to cover this completely understandable expenditure, we need to make some changes."

Then we do what should have been done all along. We reduce the defense budget by *halting* the insane pursuit of world hegemony and wasteful spending, we tax the wealthy at rates comparable to the 50s and 60s, we raise capital gains tax rates to match income tax rates, we go after the tax cheats, collect from the tax dodgers, cancel *all* unwarranted corporate subsidies, institute penalties on wild speculation by Wall Street and big banks, we introduce a transaction tax on the speculative financial industries, and so on.

We say to the oligarchs, "Sorry about that. But you wouldn't want the country to go bankrupt, would you? We *had* to do it!"

It's using their own logic on *them*, to serve the greater good of *us*.

And why shouldn't we? Don't the American people deserve it?

Is 'government of the people, by the people, for the people' just empty rhetoric?

Or should we take seriously the central premise of our experiment in self-rule?

The key here is using the Peace Dividend refund as the lever of control, the means to assert the *hegemony* of the people over their own fate. This device if it truly backs the plutocrats into a corner and contains them, will restore the power constitutionally guaranteed — the power which through the enormous accumulation of financial resources has been stolen from them — to *all* Americans. The wealthy will still have a say. But parity will prevail as originally intended. One person one vote.

Let me suggest this for those who are uncomfortable using such coercive tactics — literally wrestling from *them* the gun the oligarchs have pointed at our heads, then pointing it at theirs — weapons are neither good nor bad. It is how they are used which posits a final moral judgment. A gun used to defend the life of a child against an attacker is far different than a gun used to hold up a convenience store.

Unlike the deceptive nature of the looting done by the oligarchs — their fairy tales about how what wonderful things will accrue once they are sufficiently capitalized by the windfalls they engineer through their bought-and-paid-for lackeys in Congress — I believe wholeheartedly in the soundness and veracity of the Peace Dividend refund. I don't see it as a gambit or cleverly devised scheme for grabbing a bunch of money and handing it out arbitrarily. It is obvious that *our* tax dollars have been used for bogus and wasteful reasons. The real deception is how these wars and military expenditures have been sold to the American people. I am 100% sincere in proposing this as a legitimate payment to the American people for damages and losses incurred as a result of wars and fraudulent military allocations. I would hope that any GP/I candidate would embrace this idea with similar honest intentions and a genuine commitment to the intrinsic virtue and moral probity of the proposal.

Having said that, I believe that leveraging the Peace Dividend to gain control of the federal budget and "redistribute the wealth" — oh my god! I *said* it — though only a very small fraction of it, is just the beginning. Once the initial flood of reforms are in place and, 1) it is obvious that the result is not Armageddon, and 2) the newly-empowered citizenry get some glimpse — previews of coming attractions — of a world which is not based on unbridled greed, autocratic control by the ultra-wealthy, then we start the *real* work.

What's the real work?

Replacing a war economy with a peace economy. Substituting wherever possible cooperation for confrontation. Looking seriously at systemic reconfiguration which will immutably put people before profit.

Here are just a few specific items that come immediately to mind:

- Abolishing corporate personhood.
- Requiring incorporation at a federal level.
- Abolishing fractional reserve banking.
- Nationalizing the Federal Reserve.
- Establishing a thriving network of state banking institutions.
- Reconfiguring the entire economy toward sustainability.
- Initiating comprehensive infrastructure renewal and repair funded by *Investing in America Bonds*.
- Moving entirely from fossil fuels to clean renewables.
- Restoring quality and integrity to K-12 education.
- Guaranteeing free college education.
- Investing heavily in Earth-friendly R&D.
- 100% single-payer health care coverage.
- Giving employee-owned corporations primacy.

In terms of revitalizing democracy we might also consider:

- Calling a constitutional convention.
- Abolishing the Electoral College.
- Mandating for all federal elections — perhaps elections at all levels if possible — exclusively use countable/recountable paper ballots.

133

CHAPTER TWENTY

Bold? Outrageous?

I see it all of the time coming from the left.

A new BOLD initiative.

A BOLD groundbreaking idea.

A new BOLD strategy.

While the left keeps promising, I'm still waiting.

I'm not saying that progressives don't have *good* ideas, *admirable* values, *laudable* intentions, *worthwhile* programs, *uplifting* ideals, *inspiring* messages.

I'm saying that BOLD is not what *ever* seems to pop up these days.

I'm saying that I never see anything which grabs the public, shakes it by the shoulders, shocks them out of their coma, stirs their passions, ignites them with awe, and causes their enthusiasm glands to explode.

Of course, part of the problem is that the public is so numbed down and dumbed down.

With 5000 TV channels, the internet, streaming movies, reality shows, CSI, news and weather 24/7, they've seen it all and are rendered limp insensate lumps of ennui.

Another source of uncontrollable yawning is that many of the causes of progressives are age-old. They've been neutered by sheer repetition.

"Right. March for world peace. Like we did in the 60s?"

"Free the black man? You mean because they're all in prison?"

"Fight for women's rights? Are they going to burn their bras again?"

"Save the planet? I've been recycling soda cans for forty years now."

Same ol' same ol'.

Been there, done that.

Occupy Wall Street actually wins the award for a truly BOLD attempt at a game-changing paradigm shift within recent memory, something which seemed to come out of nowhere and blew up huge!

It definitely got the public's attention and raised its consciousness.

It spread all over the world!

From it sprang the most famous meme in recent history: *The 1% vs. the 99%!*

Which is why it was quickly and methodically destroyed by the plutocrats.

But going back before OWS, what can you think of that was truly game-changing?

Not that OWS *changed* anything. But if it hadn't been crushed, who knows?

Seriously … what can you think of that's been truly game-changing?

Thinking.

Thinking.

The Civil Rights movement?

The Feminist movement?

The Anti-Vietnam War protests?

It looks kind of bleak, doesn't it?

Being BOLD is not an easy thing to pull off.

• • •

Let's talk about my proposal of the Peace Dividend refund.

I'd say giving back *$4.52 trillion* is pretty BOLD.

I'm sure it's going to stir up quite a controversy.

After years and years of haggling over the same problems and coming up with nothing but lame non-solutions, many will be shocked indeed. Or at least taken aback.

It's so outside the box, there is no way anyone could have seen this coming.

Surely there is *no way* anyone can be neutral or indifferent.

It will provoke loud screaming pro and con.

Pro …

Alright!
Long overdue!
A breath of fresh air!
Yes! Make the 1% pay!
Finally some relief!
There is a God!

Con …

It will bankrupt the nation!
It's socialism! Communism!
Height of irresponsibility!
This is pure insanity!
It's class warfare!
Outrageous!

Outrageous?

Really?

For a government to turn to its citizenry and admit it made a mistake?

Outrageous?

135

To expect a government which found trillions of dollars to waste on fraudulent wars, bank bailouts, unnecessary military junk, to "find" the money to repay its citizens THEIR OWN MONEY is outrageous?

I don't think so.

Sure, the idea is unprecedented. Why? Because the oligarchs never give anything back. They don't even share the new wealth. They officially took $750 billion in bank and corporation bailouts. They unofficially took trillions of dollars in low-cost or free loans from the Federal Reserve, investing much of that money in sure profits, then extending their casino-style gambling with the rest of the loot, to become a more bloated and onerous burdens on the rest of us, the "unwashed masses" who are left to scramble for the table scraps and scrounge through the garbage left over from their celebrations of greed.

The economy still has not recovered, despite the fudged figures we are fed by the media.

Regular people know this. They live it every day.

Prices keep going up. Loans and interest keep piling up.

Maybe some folks who lost their jobs in the crash have gone back to work, but their new jobs pay a half or third what their old jobs paid and have no benefits.

For the 99%, the economy is a very sick patient with a gloomy prognosis for recovery.

But the good times never stopped for the 1%. They had a little setback in 2008-2009 but now the high-rollers are back to piling more wealth on top of their already incomprehensible piles of wealth, and will continue until they crash the economy again.

Whenever average Americans are hurting and the rich just keep getting richer, do they ever share the profits and gains with the average American? Everyone knows the answer to that. Income inequality is at historic highs.

To make their villainy even more insulting, as the vaults of the ultra rich corporatists bulge with more and more lucre — it is estimated that *over $40 trillion* is being horded right now, that money just sitting in shadow bank accounts across the globe *doing nothing* — these same smug traitors insist on reducing what paltry help the old, infirm, impoverished, even veterans of our wars, might get. Cut school lunches, cut education, cut social security, cut Medicare, cut unemployment benefits, cut cut cut!

Why do everyday citizens pay taxes? So the money can be squandered, so the Treasury can be looted, so corporations can get tax breaks and subsidies? Do they contribute their hard earned dollars to build unnecessary weapons, so the military can fight fraudulent wars which the public has been lied into supporting? Do we in good faith contribute toward building a strong and promising America, to then have our pay-for-play corporate boot-licker politicians tell us, *"Sorry, we're broke. We can't find the money to help the average guy anymore."* … is that why we pay taxes?

It's OUR MONEY!

It's OUR TAX DOLLARS!

Getting some fair share of the pie is scandalous? Shocking? Inconceivable?

Outrageous?

What is genuinely outrageous are the lies and spin we have to endure as our infrastructure falls apart, our young men and women in uniform die for no reason, our pensions are stolen, our federal government drowns in an ever-expanding sea of red ink, our faltering economy slips deeper into an abyss, as war follows war follows war.

The following statement is not outrageous at all.

It is sensible, just, fair, honest:

> *Examining the policies and allocations of the past 24 years, we have determined that enormous errors have been made. Approximately $4.5 trillion of tax payer money has been wasted and misappropriated. It is our duty as public servants to make redress. We are therefore refunding to each living American citizen who paid taxes between 1992 and 2015 a sum of $25,416 as compensation for the egregious mistakes in accounting, decision-making, policy formulation, and allocation.*

It would be a tragic squandering of a truly historic opportunity to demonstrate integrity and transparency in our system of government by failing the American public here, by brushing aside a chance to redress a profound injustice, while at the same time giving a much-needed and long-overdue jump-start for our floundering domestic consumer economy.

This represents a watershed moment in our history.

The *Peace Dividend* represents a momentous reversal of the self-sabotaging course America has been on for decades, a self-destructive path fraught with increasingly autocratic rule by a rich and powerful coterie of kleptocrats.

The *Peace Dividend* is the beginning of a journey that starts with America taking an honest look at itself and its citizens and saying: "We have really been screwing up. The American people deserve better."

Only GP/I candidates can make this happen.

It is incumbent on them to make it happen.

PART III:

When the candidate contracts catch fire, and especially when the *Peace Dividend* bomb drops, there will be a firestorm of biblical proportions. The juggernaut of indignation and outrage, disinformation and vilification, character assassination and condemnation from the ruling class will be vicious and relentless, cold-blooded and barbarous. It will not be pretty. It will make the dismemberment of OWS, even the witch hunt of the McCarthy era, look like Tupperware parties. The plutocrats, of course, will keep their distance. But they will unleash their armies of deception and propaganda in wave after wave: their rock star CEOs, their think tank gurus, their pay-for-play neoliberal economists, their lapdog political puppets, their bought-and-paid-for pundits and celebrity talking heads.

We must be extremely well-prepared.

What follows now are loosely-organized but tightly-crafted responses and counter-attacks to a selection of queries, objections, denunciations, rebukes and insults I believe will be hurled at GP/I candidates and proponents of the candidate contracts and the Peace Dividend proposal. Included as rejoinders are not only direct answers but diversionary tactics, feints, sometimes barbs and insults, mockery and toying.

When under fire, it is crucial to appear strong, confident, unflappable, totally in control. Being merely reasonable and coherent will not be enough. Confrontations will be as much a test of strength and will, as they are disputations of the merits of the proposals.

· · ·

Most of what follows in this section is configured in a Q&A format, the question coming from a political opponent, debate moderator, media host, aggressive news reporter, planted heckler, the answer coming from a GP/I candidate or allied spokesperson.

I also occasionally sprinkle in commentary on the *how* of my approach and the *why* of my psychology.

Yes, there is a method to it.

No, it's not original.

In fact it is time-tested and true.

To be honest, I have rarely seen this variety of tact used by progressives when presenting their case. Hence, it may at first seem foreign and unnecessarily combative. But civility and common courtesy were abandoned long ago on the political stage.

Bear in mind that typically the thrust of attacks on the GP/I will not be about challenging the message. They will be about discrediting the messenger. They will be attempts to create in the public mind the *perception* that the messenger — the GP/I candidate — is poorly informed, misguided, untrustworthy, disingenuous, desperate, just plain wrong, a fool, or completely crazy. Or harking back to my discussion of the minor party stigma, they will imply that whatever is said is irrelevant, because no minor party candidate is going to get elected to any office higher than county drain commissioner.

This is obviously not the way any intelligent, thoughtful, decent person would have it. As I've said before, we didn't create this environment, where campaigning is more like ultimate cage fighting than constructive public engagement. But wishing will not make it go away and ignoring it is a suicide pact.

There is, however, no reason to be discouraged.

Preparing for this type of "debating" just requires understanding the rules of engagement.

My advice about psychology and tactics springs from two opposite sources:

1) The mind-numbing success of the right in destroying the left: fashioning concise, compelling, persuasive messages, then staying firmly on-message, relentlessly promoting that message, maintaining iron discipline within its ranks — yes, we must sometimes learn from our enemies.

2) The equally mind-numbing blunders progressives make over-and-over in presenting their agenda to the public: the rambling, unfocused, Gordian appeals, the abstract arguments, niche messaging, the self-sabotaging disconnect with voters — yes, we must *always* learn from our own mistakes.

No one said it would be easy.

But once victory is ours, we can begin to reshape the process in ways that are more civil and respectful of the higher callings of public service and the finer quality of public servant we will then have in office.

• • •

I am entirely directing what follows at anyone who is or represents a GP/I candidate.

While I look for broad public support, it is the candidates and their supporters who will be implementing and driving the strategy.

They are the ones who will be on the firing line.

They are the ones who will be defending both their specific positions on the issues which utilize the strategy, and their use of the strategy itself.

The good news is that their highlighted policies already have — or in the case of the *Peace Dividend* will have — the support of a majority of voters. And there is a powerful logic and integrity to the strategy itself. It complements and reinforces the best aspects of real democracy.

Voter support, truth, integrity, and honorable public service are on our side.

Plus, if we do this right, we'll also have the element of surprise working in our favor. No one expects anyone in politics to tell the truth anymore.

CHAPTER TWENTY-ONE

Gotcha!

Welcome to the Age of Gotcha!

This short chapter builds on the ideas in Chapter Nine talking about sloganeering and Chapter Eleven dealing with messaging.

It sums up my advice on low and high-level harassment in any public forum, whether the annoying party is a political opponent, member of the press, media host, even a casual heckler.

'Gotcha' questions, regardless of what they specifically address, have one primary purpose. That is to humiliate, or at the very least, to knock the person being queried off stride.

There is only one effective counter to a gotcha question.

Don't answer it.

If a question is *designed* to confuse, embarrass, trap, humiliate, make you look stupid, then answering that question will only make you look confused, embarrassed, trapped, humiliated, and pathetically stupid. Duh!

Don't answer it.

There is only one way to wiggle out of the trap.

Frankly, this can be universally applied in all situations to any question that is poorly crafted, ambiguous, confusing, irrelevant, or otherwise non-productive.

Here it is …

ANSWER THE QUESTION YOU WOULD PREFER THEY HAD ASKED.

Q. How can you expect to win? Voters know voting for a third party is throwing away their vote.

[The question you would have preferred to hear: What changes in the attitudes of voters makes you confident that you will win this election?]

A. American voters are smart and understand that their vote must count. They have indeed been throwing away their votes on Republicans and Democrats for a very long time. Now that they see a winning alternative, they appreciate the power they have in the voting booth. They understand that voting for me is a vote to end the gridlock and games the two major parties have been playing. A vote for me means they will get someone to go to Washington, who is legally bound to represent their clearly stated interests.

Q. You seem to think that America is not under any serious threat. What are you going to do about ISIS and al Qaeda? Just let them overrun the country?

[The question you would have <u>preferred</u> to hear: What will guide your decisions in shaping our relations with other countries and crises we face internationally?]

A. Bill Clinton is famous for saying, "Don't make the perfect the enemy of the good." That's all well and good but I say, "Don't make the convenient the friend of the unconscionable." If we don't set our sights high, then we'll always shoot low. There is only one good reason why we are at constant war. That's because we never work hard for peace anymore. Some challenges may be so horrible and violent war is the only answer. More often than not, however, challenges are such that we can at least try to talk out our differences and resolve them peacefully. Lately, it seems like we've had leadership who can't tell the difference. Every difficulty is an excuse to drop more bombs. Not surprisingly, this results in more difficulties, creating more enemies and threats. And that predictably gives us an endless list of excuses for dropping more bombs. I've signed a contract guaranteeing the immediate safe return of our young men and women in uniform from Afghanistan. The lives and safety of Americans both here at home and abroad are my top priority.

Q. As a lunatic fringe tax-and-spend socialist, you want to destroy all of the prudent choices that have been made since the 2008 economic crash to keep our country solvent. Isn't your plan a prescription for national bankruptcy?

[The question you would have <u>preferred</u> to hear: How will your new approach to the economy foster economic growth and stability?]

A. This is not complicated and I'm surprised that you're so confused. True democracy is a wonderful and forgiving system. If it does something right, it rewards that by re-electing the people in office. If it does something wrong, it replaces them. If the voters in this district elect me, they will be saying that they do <u>not</u> see the choices that have been made as prudent at all. It means that they do not think the country is as solvent as you seem to want to believe. In terms of the economy, I have signed binding contracts which require certain actions. The voters know where I stand and what I will do on their behalf. I will work to raise the minimum wage to $15.00 per hour. I will protect Social Security and Medicare. I will fight to get their money back, and push to immediately get the Peace Dividend first refund check of $8,472 in the mail. You see, people don't care about all these labels you like to throw around. People see the problems of this country and what they see is that those problems are not getting solved. The want solutions, not fancy talk and rhetoric. Remedies, not labels. If I'm elected, the voice and collective wisdom of the American people will be clear. The message will be that _my_ _program_ is what they believe will truly foster economic growth and financial solvency. Are you going to argue with the voters then? Are you going to call the majority of voters in this district a bunch of lunatic fringe socialists?

Q. Some are calling you just a modern day Robin Hood. What do you say to those who accuse you of stealing from the rich to give to the poor?

[The question you would have _preferred_ to hear: How can you justify refunding $4.52 trillion to taxpayers in the form of what you call the Peace Dividend? Doesn't this unfairly target the rich?]

A. I guess the first question we need to ask is who is stealing what from whom. Let's say you buy something and when you get it home you discover it doesn't work. You take it back and demand a refund. Are robbing the store? The rich are now running this country. Regular citizens have no say in what their government does. Regular folks still have to pay taxes but they get no voice in how that tax money is spent. It's taxation without representation all over again. We have documented that for the past 24 years over $4.52 trillion dollars was wasted, literally thrown out the window. This is a conservative estimate of the malfeasance and fraud which squandered the hard-earned tax dollars contributed by everyday citizens. Government has been broken. All I'm saying is we the people deserve our money back. We deserve a refund for what has turned out to be a very defective product. Since the rich have been in charge, yes, they bear the responsibility for the disastrous decisions. The unnecessary wars, the pork barrel defense projects for military equipment that doesn't work or we don't need. But the money belongs to the American people, not just a few rich folks at

143

the top. I don't see any Robin Hood operating here. I see honesty. I see government admitting its mistakes and making amends.

I could go on. But the methodology is clear.

As discussed in Chapter Eleven, *Messaging*, it's about controlling the conversation, shaping the narrative in terms that carries *our* message, the essential building blocks of the GP/I candidate's campaign.

• • •

Remember, every public appearance is an opportunity for driving home the central themes of a GP/I candidate.

Even harassment can be turned around and used as yet another propitious occasion for effectively delivering the message that the GP/I candidate wants heard.

Especially a rude gotcha question.

It's perfect! Everyone is paying attention!

They want to see, perhaps with a degree of sadistic relish, what the GP/I candidate is going to say and do.

Loaded questions, even broadside ad hominem attacks can be capitalized on in two ways.

First, by redirecting the narrative, essential message content can be shared. Just following the simple, straightforward advice above gets the job done.

ANSWER THE QUESTION YOU WOULD
PREFER THEY HAD ASKED.

Second, by remaining firm, in-control, decisive, focused, the GP/I candidate demonstrates he or she can take the heat, has the right stuff, is clever, strong and determined.

This proof of character — this surviving these trials by media fire in public forums and coming out on top — are as important as the content of policy positions to the average voter, because passing the test offers assurance that the GP/I candidate has the strength and endurance to drive his or her policy commitments to a successful conclusion. Being strong under pressure inspires confidence and trust.

CHAPTER TWENTY-TWO

Q & A: Minor Parties and
Candidate Contracts

The next several chapters jump head first into the war of words.

I am attempting here to give some very concrete advice.

But just as importantly, to illustrate an attitude, a carriage, a self-confidence, which readies the GP/I candidate for what's to come.

While we can hope for the best, we must be prepared for the worst.

I suspect that if the public starts clamoring for the major party candidate to sign legally binding contracts, or if the idea of the *Peace Dividend* catches fire — which neither Democrats or Republicans can *possibly* get behind — a major war will break out and GP/I candidates across the board will be targeted for termination. We can expect the attack dogs, both the established politicos and their mercenary media shock troops, to launch a major offensive, consisting of smug vilification, patronizing mockery, outright condemnation, and merciless character assassination.

Purely for survival, it's absolutely necessary to be prepared.

Dress for battle or get crushed.

Remember, properly fending off often stupid, rude, and even ad hominem attacks results in two outstanding and highly laudable rewards: 1) it will give dignity and credibility to any GP/I who can pull it off, and 2) it gives substance and weight to the ideas, it fleshes them out, and the sheer repetition of important themes will start to seed in a wary public mind the sense that there *is* something to this very different message after all.

Let's get started by looking at attacks on the viability of minor party candidates and the use of candidate contracts.

The questions come from political opponents, newspaper reporters, media hosts, panel moderators, members of the audience, dog Spot, Max Headroom.

• • •

Q. This smacks of an assault on the time-tested two-party system. What gives you the right to challenge and attempt to undermine the parties that have delivered so much over decades?

A. The major parties each have long records of accomplishment. For this they should be recognized and lauded. But all that good stuff ended when vast piles of money entered the system and destroyed

145

representative government. The two major parties undermined themselves when they stopped listening to the people and started only listening to big banks, Wall Street, and the ultra rich.

For the record, we have always had many political parties. There are many parties now. This is nothing new. The only relevant question is, which parties, whether we're talking one, two, three, or ninety, best represents the will of the voters. This is our system. It's called democracy.

Let me add this, in case you weren't paying attention in history class. When Lincoln was elected in 1860, there were *four* major parties. FOUR ... the Southern Democratic Party, the Constitutional Union Party, the Democratic Party, and the Republican Party. If four parties was good enough for Lincoln, it's good enough for us, don't you think?

Q. Everybody knows what happens when a third party gets in the fray. Ralph Nader mucked things up so badly, the Florida vote ended up in the Supreme Court. Why should anyone throw away their vote by voting for you?

A. What planet are you on? Everyone knows that the election of 2000 was stolen. I have to hand it to the Republicans. They threw tens of thousands of Democrats off the voting registers, closed down the recount, got their right wing buddies on the Supreme Court to hand down one of the most abominable rulings in the history of jurisprudence, then managed to blame Al Gore's defeat on Ralph Nader. Quite an accomplishment.

At the end of the day, it all comes down to arithmetic. If the majority of voters in this particular race decide they want me to represent them, how will that be throwing be throwing votes away? It sounds like democracy at work to my ears.

Q. I'm not getting this whole candidate contract thing. The system has worked for over two hundred years. Why introduce some unnecessary new process, some legalistic hocus-pocus to complicate matters?

A. People used horses for thousands of years. There came a time when a hay wagon or a carriage wasn't up to the task. Maybe there was a time when a man's word was good enough. But apparently those

146

days are over. Every election cycle, the promises fly around like butterflies in spring, but after election day most of those promises — certainly the important ones — mysteriously disappear and are never heard from again. So it looks like we need something more substantial, more binding than a politician's word now. There are lies, damn lies, and campaign speeches.

There's nothing extreme about the idea of a candidate contract. Let me ask you this: Would you sell your house to someone who promised on just a handshake to pay you? How about if someone wanted to borrow $10,000 from you? Wouldn't you get it in writing?

I say to any voter out there. If a candidate won't sign on the dotted line, he doesn't deserve your vote. Promises are nice but save them for New Years resolutions. If you hire someone to remodel your house, you get a contract. If you decide to take an expensive vacation, you get it all in writing. If you take out a loan to buy a car, the terms are in black and white. How is it different with your elected representative? You're sending someone representing your interests, writing laws, protecting you, setting up tax codes, deciding how your tax dollars are spent. This is important stuff. It impacts every aspect of your life. Demand it in writing. There's nothing strange or unprecedented about it. I agree that it's a shame it's come to this. But it's the politicians themselves who have spoiled things. The honor system required honoring one's word, keeping campaign promises, being honorable. Too many broken promises have broken that system.

Q. About these candidate contracts. This sounds like coercion. Blackmail. You're telling voters that if a candidate won't sign these contracts, he should be run out of office?

A. Nobody's forcing anyone to do anything. If you want to work as a carpenter, you have to use a hammer. If you refuse, no one will hire you. It's your choice. Voters want firm commitments from their elected officials. If a candidate won't guarantee certain action by signing a contract, the voters will hire someone else. Sign or don't sign. It's the candidate's free choice.

And frankly, calling this blackmail just shows your lack of vocabulary. Yes, it's an ultimatum. Either start representing the people and doing what they want, or find a different career. It's like any other job. If I wanted to work at McDonald's but refused to make French fries or wear the hat with the McDonald's logo, I wouldn't get the job. If a politician is being elected to represent the interests of his or her constituents but would rather do what his rich campaign donors or powerful lobbyists want, then that politician doesn't get the job. Maybe he could work at McDonald's.

Q. Are these contracts even legal?

A. They are as legal as any contract between two parties. Those parties can be individuals or classes of people. Our contract is simple. It commits a political candidate to perform certain desired actions. If once in office he or she fails to fulfill the obligations, it gives the constituents legal redress. If the politician breaks his commitment, a huge penalty is imposed via a class action lawsuit and that money is shared as damages among the class of individuals which constitutes his or her constituency. Every voter gets a check for the elected official's negligence, for the damage that the malfunctioning politician has inflicted on the congressional district.

Q. You propose "class action" penalties for breach of the candidate contract. Is there even a legal precedent for such an outrageous idea?

A. I guess you never go to the movies. The movie "Erin Brockovich" told the underlying story for one of the largest class action lawsuits in U.S. history. PG&E knowingly violated the public trust and the residents of Hinckley, California were awarded $333 million. PG&E materially harmed the health and well-being of the community by dumping a known carcinogen into the water supply.

Similarly, if a candidate knowingly violates the explicit terms of the candidate contract he or she signed, there is a violation of the public trust and an award of damages will be sought on behalf of the voters. It's a very hefty penalty, quite intentionally so. $10 million per violation on specific issues, and $50 million for failure to resign from office as stipulated in the contract. These candidate contracts are nothing to be taken lightly.

Q. Mr. *[name of opponent]*, the Republican incumbent in this election just signed a similar contract for protecting Social Security. Why shouldn't voters send him back to Washington?

A. He should sign something, that's for sure. Mr. *[name of opponent]*'s voting record on Social Security is appalling.

148

But he didn't sign *[holding up candidate contract]* <u>this</u> contract.

Please do yourself and the public an enormous service and read the fine print. You will see that the document Mr. *[name of opponent]* signed is in no way comparable. If he is trying to pull the wool over the eyes of the public, then I say, shame on him. If however, this is just the product of an obtuse sense of humor, we can just dismiss it as a bad joke.

In either case, people aren't being fooled. You see, American voters are smart. They see these tricks and publicity stunts for what they are.

By the way, everyone is welcome to visit my website where the real candidate contract *[again holding up candidate contract]* is right beside the fake contract that Mr. *[name of opponent]* is peddling. The differences are obvious. But everyone can judge for themselves.

Q. So let's say people in this district buy into this whole contract scam and you get elected. You're just one person. So what if you go in and sponsor legislation. It'll still get defeated. Why isn't that for the people of this district throwing away their vote?

A. People are fed up with business-as-usual. Congressional approval rating is down around 8%, an all-time low. Maybe you haven't been paying attention, but I'm one of many across this entire nation who are one-by-one taking back our government. Candidates from coast-to-coast in every district are carrying this message to the voters. We've all signed legally binding contracts, so the voters will finally get the representation in Washington DC they deserve, the representation that's been missing for decades.

The American public is waking up. They see now that the best way to throw away a vote is voting for the say-one-thing-do-another Democrats and Republicans who have created the mess we're in.

CHAPTER TWENTY-THREE

Q & A: The Peace Dividend

Since this is probably the most controversial proposal since someone suggested the colonies break with the King and go it alone, it will likely generate the most heat.

Therefore, its defense must be the most unassailable.

I highly favor a strategy of counter-attack, counter-intimidation — fight fire with fire.

• • •

Q. Aren't you just buying votes with this Peace Dividend scheme?

A. That's laughable coming from anyone who supports the current two-party system. Money has completely corrupted our democracy. Lobbyists run with fistfuls of corporate dollars through Congress "buying votes" every day. Campaign contributions for the last election cycle totaled $3.7 billion. *$3.7 billion!*

Since *you* brought up buying votes, let's see how this plays out. I'll give one example. 93% of American voters want GMO labeling of their foods. Monsanto is the industry leader in terms of developing and marketing GMO food items and vehemently opposes labeling. Monsanto to date has spent over $82 million lobbying legislators. It has recently contributed over $16 million to federal candidates. 93% of Americans want GMO labeling, yet legislation has been defeated over and over. So who is buying votes?

But to directly address your question. Tax payers fund the government. The money belongs to the citizens of this country. It's their money. If you buy a defective appliance and take it back to the store where you bought it, you get your money back. We are doing the same thing. The public has been given broken goods for over two decades. We're giving them the money back. If the voters elect me, it is my responsibility to do the job they ask me to do, starting with the Peace Dividend refund. I have signed a contract with the voters on this and will honor that legal commitment.

Q. You're saying with a straight face that you promise to send over $25,000 to each and every taxpaying citizen and you claim you're not buying their votes?

A. And you're saying with a straight face that the people we elected to office should ignore the needs of the American people and hand over the wealth of the country to the 1%, export our good jobs, give tax breaks to corporations, let criminals who have looted the Treasury and stolen the tax dollars of good decent citizens go free, promote endless wars, and waste trillions on defective military equipment?

What kind of American are you to support the destruction of democracy? What kind of American are you to stand by and watch good, decent people suffer while billionaires party like there's no tomorrow?

I know what kind of Americans listen to and respect what I have to say. They are the kind of people who struggle to makes ends meet while the government throws away the money they in good faith pay every April 15th, then comes back for more.

Maybe you should do your homework. I know this is asking a lot. But just read the specific language of the Peace Dividend. It's all there in black-and-white. If you have trouble understanding it, just ask any 10-year-old kid who lives in your neighborhood to explain it to you.

Q. Apparently you want to bankrupt the American government.

A. Well, isn't that ironic. That's like a murderer standing over the dead body and saying to the police who just arrived on the scene, "You've apparently come here to kill this man!"

Our misleadership has already nearly bankrupted the American economy with its endless wars, its giveaways of tax dollars to your corporate sponsors, its allowing its deep-pocketed campaign donors to loot the treasury, its incentivizing the shipping of jobs overseas, its protecting billionaires who hide their skyscraper-high stacks of money in secret accounts in tax havens all over the world. And you're accusing *me* of wanting to bankrupt the government?

All I want to do is take back the trillions of dollars the two major parties have stolen from the American people and return it to the rightful owners. Give a refund to the American people so they can spend it back into the economy, create jobs here at home. Instead of throwing money to the wind and squandering it in every *other* country, Americans can put that money to work for America, in their schools, right here at home repairing roads and bridges in their own communities, where they work and live, not in Baghdad or Kiev or Kabul.

Q. You're actually with a straight face going to stand behind this slick campaign gimmick of raiding the treasury and giving away trillions of dollars? This is the height of irresponsibility!

A. Well, isn't that interesting! Irresponsible, eh? According to the dictionary, being irresponsible in the context of public service means failing to fulfill an obligation to do something, incapable of being trusted, and not being morally accountable for one's behavior.

So you have these incumbent politicians lie through their teeth to get elected, then turn around and fail to fulfill their obligation to serve their constituents, elected officials who conveniently forget their campaign promises, who forget why they were elected, who clearly can't be trusted to follow through, seem to have no pangs of conscience about lying to the public, saying one thing but doing another, elected officials who never show the slightest remorse for being so lousy at their jobs, and who never even apologize for deceiving the people who put them in office.

And you're saying I'm being irresponsible because I'm offering to sign a binding contract which specifies openly and honestly what I will do when elected? You're saying I'm being irresponsible for acknowledging the enormously costly mistakes that have been made, the vast sums of taxpayer money which has been wasted? You're saying that I'm being irresponsible for saying to the public, this was your money and you deserve either to get what you paid for or get your money back? It seems like you need to go back to school and learn what words like 'irresponsible' actually mean.

• • •

There's a method here. Whenever possible, GP/I candidates need to parry these kinds of attacks by using the words of the accuser, turning the language around and making it obvious that *they* are the ones guilty of their allegations, aspersions and innuendos, citing in straightforward, sincere, vivid language honest examples of how *they* betray the public interest, how *they* are actually the culpable parties.

• • •

Q. You've referred at points to this giveaway to the taxpayer as 'war reparations'. In what sense can you construe this as war reparations? War against who?

A. From what I've seen, not only have the previous administrations been at war with a host of other countries, but they've been at war with the average American citizen, *and* certainly at war with the truth. Lie after lie has been dangled before the American public. People have been unconscionably railroaded into a state of panic, subjected to all sorts of fear mongering and outright deceptions. Not only that, but money that should have gone to benefit average Americans has been squandered on all sorts of misadventures, or handed over to the already ultra-wealthy.

What would you call it when the truth takes a back seat and when average Americans get beaten down constantly with lousy jobs, unemployment and underemployment? What would you call it when fine young men and women in the spring of youth, get sent to fight stupid and unnecessary wars? What do you have to say to the parents and loved ones of the 6,000 young men and women who in honorable and patriotic service to our country got killed in Afghanistan and Iraq, two wars which *didn't* have to be fought? What do you say to the 50,897 maimed and disabled? To the 290,000 who suffer from PTSD? Gee, we're sorry?

I know exactly what to call it.

For quite some time the ruling elites have been at war with the average citizen. These spoiled, rich plutocrats don't care. Which is why <u>we the people</u> must. We can't bring our fallen soldiers back to life, we can't put eyes back in heads, we can't sew legs back on, but the least we can do is offer some small financial relief in the form of reparations, to the millions of Americans who have suffered under this regime of domestic terror, the ongoing gross and inhumane mistreatment of the average citizen. The American people deserve to live in peace and at peace. They deserve whatever

153

they have coming for the last two-and-a-half decades of war. War on the middle class. War on the young. War on the less fortunate. War on good, decent taxpaying citizens.

Q. This will bankrupt the country. How can you suggest make an outrageous proposal? Where will the $4.5 trillion come from?

A. You're familiar with the incredible, awe-inspiring history of this country, and you can still ask such a question? What an insult to every single proud American? Ever heard of American ingenuity? We're a country that has taken on some of the toughest challenges in history and found a way. Now you're saying that the most powerful country in the world, the most successful nation in the entire history of the human race, America which by a huge margin has the biggest economy on the planet, can't figure this out?

Sure, it's a lot of money. But let me ask you this. Before we blew $1.5 trillion on the completely unnecessary wars in Afghanistan and Iraq, where was the money? Before we threw away $398 billion on the F-35 boondoggle, where was the money? Did we have a $2 trillion dollars stacked up in a warehouse and so we said, *"Gosh, we need to spend this so let's start a war. And while we're at it, we'll build a plane that can't fly in the rain."* No, we didn't have the money sitting around. But we managed to find the money so we could put it to <u>bad use</u>. So now we need to find money to put to <u>good use</u>! We have legitimate things that need to get done, things which are good for the American people and will help put our faltering economy back on the road to recovery, and it's: *"Oh no! Gosh, we can't afford to do that. No, we need to wait and figure out something else, more wars like Iraq and Afghanistan. Or I know, maybe we can build a big incinerator in the desert and put everyone's hard-earned tax dollars in it and really get the job done right."*

Putting aside your cavalier and nearly treasonous dismissal of America as some third-rate country that isn't up to the task, a nearly treasonous indictment of America as incapable of meeting a challenge and doing something good for its own people for a change, let me tell you something. And this goes out to everybody who will come out of the cracks and whine like you did, *"We can't afford it!"*. I want all you nay-sayers listen up: We *can* do this. We *will* do this. It's the right thing to do! The people — you remember the people, don't you? Well, this country belongs to the people. Tax

154

money belongs to the people. And the people owe it to themselves to get back the money that was stolen from them and wasted. We will find the $4.52 trillion and we'll put it to good use, helping families with their mortgages and car payments, their children's education, helping people pay down their debts, all the money they've borrowed to survive because the economy was trashed by these ridiculous, immoral, unnecessary wars and buying military junk.

The war reparation payment of $25,516 really doesn't begin to cover the losses. But it's a start. I'm willing to at least begin addressing this injustice. Literally, this theft of their hard-earned dollars. I'm willing to say to the American people, "I'm sorry for this. You deserve better. Here's some of the money the U.S. government owes you for making such a mess of things."

This is good government. This is government *for* the people. All of the people.

What's outrageous about that?

Q. You can put a fancy spin on your handout, but isn't it just socialism?

A. Actually, it's Christianity, it's Judaism, it's Islam. I quote …

> Thus saith the LORD: I, the Lord, command you to do what is just and right. Protect the person who is being cheated from the one who is cheating him.

That's from the Bible, Jeremiah 22:3. Another one from the Bible …

> Let no one seek his own good, but the good of his neighbor.

That's 1 Corinthians 10:24. These are from the Koran …

> Among those We have created there is a community who guide by the Truth and act justly according to it. (Surat al-A 'raf, 181)

> Say: My Lord has commanded justice … (Surat al-A 'raf, 29) … if you do judge, judge between them justly. (Surat al-Maida, 42)

For those of you out there who are atheists and agnostics, there's a name for it what we're doing. It's called COMMON DECENCY.

Q. You've been talking in a lot of generalities. Do you actually have a plan or are you just blowing smoke?

A. We have the best minds in America determining what needs to be done to pay back the money the American people are owed for the idiocy of the last twenty-four years. The detailed plan is complete and will be made available at the appropriate time.

In broad strokes, I can say this.

We will shrink government where necessary and prudent, we will rewrite the tax laws, we will close tax loopholes, end wasteful subsidies, we will take back under the auspices of the Department of the Treasury the creation and control of the nation's currency, and lastly we will issue *Peace Bonds* in affordable denominations, which will raise capital and allow Americans themselves, if they so choose, to invest in a prosperous and peaceful future.

We will also be issuing infrastructure bonds, called *Investing In America Bonds*, so that Americans can directly invest in a comprehensive renewal of their country.

Each tax payer in receiving their $25,416 Peace Dividend will have the option of putting any portion of that in either *Peace Bonds* or *Investing In America Bonds*, so that if they choose, their Peace Dividend refund can become an investment in America, which will pay them handsomely over the long term. This is purely optional, of course.

Q. Are you accusing our leaders of being corrupt? Are you accusing them of fraud?

A. We now has a system of inverted justice in this country. An investment banker can misuse depositor funds, lie to the banks stockholders, lose billions of dollars in casino-style playing the market, engage in fraud and misrepresentation, and go completely free, plus get a generous performance bonus for his excellent work. But some young guy who had his job sent to China or Vietnam, is

156

down on his luck, and gets caught stealing a carton of milk for his kids, plea bargains his way to three years in prison.

All I know is that if I have anything to say about it, this is going to stop.

As for corruption in Congress and other institutions of government, I think the record speaks for itself. It is up to the courts to decide if any of our public servants have committed crimes or run afoul of anti-corruption laws. I will say that purely from a common sense perspective, grave injustices have been perpetrated. The resulting losses that good, decent Americans have incurred must be somehow compensated.

We'll start with the Peace Dividend, which is a direct refund for collection and misuse of taxpayer money for military and war, and go from there.

I have signed several binding contracts spelling out exactly what I am required to do from my first day in office. I intend to meet those obligations with due diligence.

CHAPTER TWENTY-FOUR

Q & A: Economic Issues

Many Americans actually feel that the economy has steadily improved since the 2008 crash. Though this belief often runs contrary to their own personal experience — prices are up, wages are stagnant, earning power is decreasing, debt continues to pile up, many are underemployed or have just given up even trying to find a job — riding on a wish and a prayer, they accept the fudged and cherry-picked statistics of the government, but also remain heedful of warnings that the recovery is fragile and we should do nothing risky, stay the course, and hope for the best.

Of course, the stark reality is things are getting worse and America is still in a long, slow, steady decline.

That's exactly how the 1% like it. They cash in on the systemic dysfunction. The rest of us suffer.

Anyone who attempts to remedy any of the injustices against the majority of Americans will get the same old tired arguments and twisted logic. Why not? They've been working quite nicely for a long time now.

• • •

Q. You want to increase social security. But many respected economists say that Social Security is bankrupt. Now you're talking about increasing it? Isn't that irresponsible or insane?

A. Social security is not bankrupt and it never will be. For starters, we won't let it go bankrupt. People should understand that this talk of bankruptcy comes from the sinister and cynical investment class, who want to "privatize" the most successful social program in America's history. What does that mean? That's simple. Social Security is the biggest single pile of money sitting around right now. What we have is not a bankrupt system. What we have and what the investment bankers see is a very big pile of money, which by the way belongs to the American people. Every working American has put their hard-earned dollars into what is effectively a savings account, let me repeat, a retirement savings account of *their* money. There are bankers and hedge funds who want to get their hands on that all of that money. They want to "privatize" it, which is fancy talk for taking it over, putting on their books instead of the safe and secure books of the U.S. government.

We've noticed for some time now that whenever there is a big pile of money in a program that the bankers want, just coincidentally, well-paid economists pop us and declare, *"Oh my, that program is insolvent! It's tottering on the brink of bankruptcy!"* The bankers, of course, are glad to rescue it. Out of the goodness of their hearts, naturally.

People of America, listen up. Social Security is your money. Don't let anyone fool you. Social Security is not broke. Your benefits will be there. Don't let the banksters steal it the way they've robbed the U.S. Treasury now for two decades, with their bailouts and handouts and interest free loans.

I signed a binding contract, so I will go to Washington DC and safeguard the investment all Americans have made in their retirement. I believe — no, let me correct that — I *know* we can do better by our seniors. By managing Social Security properly, implementing more equitable policies for funding it, I know we can *increase* benefits and keep the system stable and solvent. *Forever!*

Q. Your radical ideas for paying for this war reparations hoax includes other nefarious items. What's this about nationalizing the Fed? Or imposing a transaction tax on Wall Street?

A. Each candidate is required, as I am required, to deliver on those items specified in whatever candidate contracts are signed. Here in my district, I have agreed to fight the people's fight to protect Social Security and Medicare, finally bring home our troops from Afghanistan, raise the minimum wage to $15 per hour, end unnecessary oil and other industry subsidies, and as you've alluded to, to push for the Peace Dividend refund package to return to taxpayers some of the money the Pentagon has blown.

What happens after that is subject to discussion. While you would like to engage in wild speculation and get the public riled up about nothing, our approach is different. It's different in two ways.

First, we will be listening to the voters. If the American people think a transaction tax is a good idea, that's what we'll push for. If the American people are sick of the abuses of privilege by the

Federal Reserve, we will figure out together what should be done. Nothing is written in stone.

The second way our approach is different is why the candidate contracts came about in the first place. American voters are tired of being promised one thing, then once the election is over, the promises get broken. Our current political leaders stopped listening to their constituents and now only listen to their wealthy sponsors, the deep-pocketed rich and powerful, who contribute mountains of money into getting those same leaders elected.

We will continue listening to the people, our constituents who entrust us with the responsibility of representing their interests when we go to Washington.

If the people think the Fed should be nationalized, that's what we'll do. But we sure aren't going to ask the Fed and all of the people who have a financial stake in its future what to do. That's like asking drunk drivers to write the laws governing drunk driving.

We intend to institute something which hasn't been seen for quite some time in this country: government by the people, of the people, for the people. I love that! It has a great ring to it, don't you think?

Q. You claim we need to protect Medicare. It seems to be working just fine. What is there to protect? Against what or who?

A. It's working fine for the pharmaceutical companies, that's for sure. Why is it that prescription drugs are 35% to 45% lower in Canada than in the U.S.?

Why is it that heart-bypass surgery costs 85% less in Canada than in the U.S.?

Why is it that the % of GDP spent on health care in Canada is 11% while in the U.S. it is 17%?

The answer to your question is right there. We need to protect Medicare from excessive costs, from exploitation by our corporatized health care system, just as we have to protect each individual citizen from runaway costs and exploitation. Why do the health care providers charge excessively for their services? Because they can.

160

If this sort of abuse continues because we don't have the basic common sense to put some limits and restraints on this profiteering, Medicare will be bankrupted by greed.

Q. Study after study shows that America is an unfriendly environment for business and becoming more so. Now you propose raising the minimum wage to at least $15 per hour. Are you trying to drive businesses out of the country? Won't they just go to someplace where they can find cheaper labor?

A. Do you have any clue how absurd that last question is? There are millions of jobs that simply cannot be moved overseas. If my car breaks down and I need a tow truck, are they going to have road service come from Vietnam because the drivers there work for less? Will they bus my kids to Bangladesh in the morning because teachers only get 35 cents an hour there?

And by the way, I can show you study after study that shows a higher minimum wage is *better* for domestic businesses. When people make better wages, they can buy more. Maybe they can actually afford to eat at the restaurant where they work. Or buy a car from the dealership where they clean the offices or work in the service department.

One of the healthiest, most profitable major corporate box store chains is Costco. The average wage there is over $21 per hour. Each store has loyal, knowledgeable employees. They work hard and get paid well. People love to shop at Costco because the employees are cheerful, helpful and knowledgeable. Everyone wins.

Q. You claim that corporations need to start paying their fair share. That exploiting tax loopholes and off-shoring operations will no longer allow them to skip out on paying. Why should the corporations put up with this? Won't they just stop doing business here and America will lose even more commerce to overseas markets?

A. Let's ask *your* own question another way to demonstrate the absurdity of what you're suggesting. Apple has sold almost 60 million iPhones in America. Their total revenue for sales in the U.S. last year was over $5 billion. That's for *one year*. So you're asking: If the U.S. government demands they pay 35% corporate taxes for

161

the privilege of selling their products here, why won't Apple have a hissy fit and storm off, refusing to sell anything here? Isn't this what you're question implies?

These huge multinational corporations are not run by school children who throw a tantrum when something cuts into their profits a bit. The only reason Apple *doesn't* pay taxes on enormous chunks of their earnings is simple: *We don't require them to!*

Because we don't require them to give back to the country where they not only got their start, but got a ton of the technology that goes into their products, they have $178 billion in the bank sitting around doing nothing. They are the richest corporate entity on the planet. That cash alone — not the value of Apple which is over $760 billion, but just the cash laying around — is greater than the Gross National Product of 132 countries! I'd say they're doing alright.

Apple has thousands of stores here and do a vast amount of business in the U.S. Requiring them to pay more of their earnings back into the national community which supports and promotes their growth and success is hardly an unreasonable request.

That's just one spectacular example. The point is, the vast wealth of hundreds of mega-corporations were built on the backs of hard-working Americans, using the research and development of government agencies, using the security and stability of America to develop and market their products, using American labor to build their initial products before they shipped the jobs to China. So to expect them to pay some fair share of their earnings back to the nation which fostered their growth is hardly asking too much.

Those companies who took all this and ran somewhere else to avoid paying taxes will be first on the list to come clean and ante up. It's only fair. It's the right thing to do.

Q. You talk about creating jobs. For the past eight years we've seen how difficult this is. What makes you think you have all the answers? How exactly are you going to create jobs?

A. Now listen carefully or you might miss this. We're going to create jobs by creating jobs. The private sector has destroyed high paying jobs, shipped jobs overseas, then has half-heartedly and ineffectively replaced some those lost jobs with ones which pay half as much.

We can't wait around any longer. There's work to be done in this country. Lots of it. We're going to hire people at good wages and get the work done.

It's called the direct approach. Works every time.

CHAPTER TWENTY-FIVE

Q & A: Defense Policy and
Fighting Terrorism

Let's hear it for the fear card.

Ready? One two three …

TERRORISM!

I know no other way of dealing with this that beating it to death with a big club. The bigger the club, the more ferocious the attack, the better.

Kill it! Dig a hole! Bury it!

Americans may be finally getting fear-weary anyway.

Many are getting the uneasy feeling that something is seriously wrong.

That America is unraveling.

That America is unraveling from the inside.

Not from being attacked by al Qaeda, ISIS, Russia. Not from being infected by Ebola.

But by being infected by its own lunacy!

The War On Terror has had a good run. Over 14 years and counting. People have been brainwashed, trained to be very afraid, cower behind the apron of their big daddy government protector. Patriotism has been equated to living in fear 24/7.

Granted, it's not going to be easy to undo much of the conditioning, the damage to our collective psyches, the mutilation of our sense of security, the shattering if our self-confidence, the false hyper-inflation of our vulnerability.

They did a real number on us!

But as in many such scenarios, the best defense is an offense.

In fact, I can't think of many issues where this advice is more germane than in challenging the whole War On Terror, with its obvious mass deceptions, ubiquitous web of fear, and consequent gutting of the sense of rugged individualism which has historically been the hallmark of our national character.

Just expect a very dirty fight. There's a lot of money at stake.

• • •

Q. Are you saying it's wrong to fight terrorism?

A. I'm saying that the way we've gone about it has been a total waste of taxpayer money. We are losing the war on terrorism. We have created terrorists. We had a few crackpots in 2001 with some wire cutters. Now the world is swarming with well-armed bands of jihadist lunatics. The NSA, DOD, CIA and Homeland Security have been trying to put out a fire by pouring gasoline on it.

So here's the plan. The first thing we need to do is make amends to the American people for throwing their hard-earned money down the drain. That money could have been put to work here at home making *America* stronger, creating jobs, repairing roads, making our schools better. Instead, we used it to blow up buildings in Iraq, so we could waste more money building them new ones. Is this supposed to make sense?

Next, while we're giving that money back to American citizens so they can get on with their lives, we go back to the drawing board and figure out how to *actually* fight terrorism and make our country safe again from all of the *new terrorists* we have created. At the same time, we start addressing those specific things which foster the growth of terrorism.

There are solutions to all this, you know. There is so much we haven't tried because we've been so busy bombing and droning. And we start with identifying the real enemies of America, the ones who are sponsoring all of this. We look at what it is that we are doing to perpetuate and promote the agenda of these hostile forces. We reverse course.

That is not the same as surrendering.

It's taking the initiative doing what needs to be done, not just react like a bunch of kids in a schoolyard fight.

Q. You're accusing the U.S. government of creating the terrorists?

A. I am saying that U.S. meddling and bad judgment has created the *environment* out of which these terrorist organizations grow. I am saying that often we are our own worst enemy. Two perfect examples.

1) We funded Osama bin Laden, gave him arms and support to fight in Afghanistan because we didn't like the government back then. That group of disorganized, ragtag jihadists became al Qaeda, which turned against the U.S. You know the rest of the story.

2) We funded and supported Saddam Hussein back in the 1980s. Then we decided he was getting too big for his britches and we destroyed Iraq. The soldiers we "defeated" then went on to form ISIS. They hate the U.S. They didn't before but we turned them into our enemies. Now they've captured tons of military equipment we put in Iraq and build an army bent on revenge. They're destroying the Middle East with *American* military equipment!

The capper to this madcap story is ISIS now taunts the U.S., begging us to bomb them because they know it will help them recruit new jihadists. So what do we do? We bomb them. Now that's brilliant, eh? Guess what? ISIS is growing in numbers and strength. The more we bomb them, the stronger they grow. This is so dumb it wouldn't fly as a Saturday morning cartoon show. Kids are smarter than that.

If you don't see a problem here with what we're doing, try banging your head against a wall because it feels so good.

Q. So you would have *cut* the defense budget after 9/11?

A. Cutting or increasing is not the choice. The choice is spending wisely or throwing taxpayer money away by buying worthless military systems and making horrible foreign policy decisions. If the trillions of dollars we've spent have not been a complete waste, then why do we have more wars going on than ever?

Look at the realities. The more we spend, the more we arm the world, the more conflict and aggression there is. The bloating of the defense budget is no accident. It runs in perfect parallel with the bloating of the defense industries. War is profit. More war is more profit. This makes America less, not more safe.

A strong defense starts with a strong America. A strong America starts at home, with each and every American citizen, each American family, each American community.

A strong defense is not trying to bomb away every problem. You can't bomb your way to peace. Our current foreign policy is only good for embalmers and casket makers, cemeteries and crematoriums.

The American people are smart. They're beginning to see through all of this. They're waking up to the fact that they've been lied to and conned into the mess we're in. If I can paraphrase from the 1978 movie *Network*: Americans are mad as hell and they aren't going to take it anymore!

Q. You're saying ISIS is not a threat? Aren't they beheading people and running amok all over the Middle East?

A. ISIS is a threat to many people in the Middle East. But so is Saudi Arabia, which makes a public display of beheading sixty to eighty people every year, for crimes like peaceful political dissent.

However, if you're so afraid of ISIS, I'll give you my word. When I'm elected, if ISIS shows up in your neighborhood, just call me directly and I'll have our finest fighting men and women in uniform surround your house and keep you safe. They'll be there within fifteen minutes. Promise.

Before that happens, however, I plan on cutting off all funding to ISIS, cutting off all arms shipments to ISIS, and sanctioning any country, whether an ally of the United States or not, who is giving ISIS material support. *That* will do more to stop them in their tracks than even putting boots on the ground. If they don't have weapons to fire and can't put gas in their SUVs and military trucks, they're not going to be able to do much, eh?

• • •

A huge part of pulling off these answers is attitude and posturing! It's about being so totally cocksure, it's as if the person who asked the question is unbelievably out of touch.

"Of course we didn't need to attack Iraq! Where have you been? The American people know this. Everybody knows this!"

It's about creating a feeling of camaraderie with the public. They sense the GP/I's absolute certainty, his or her confidence in speaking on their behalf and standing up to these idiots who want to continue trying to bamboozle them. People don't like to be played for fools. The GP/I must with grace and gravity let them know they have an ally, someone who knows what's truly going on, what the stakes are, and is right there ready to stand strong and put a halt to the flimsy lies and propaganda.

"You would like us to think you know what you're doing. But the American people can spot incompetence a mile away. The War On Terror has accomplished nothing except make more enemies. Join the human race. Grow some brains. Get a clue!"

Attitude!

• • •

Q. It's obvious that you want to gut the military and weaken America.

A. I think you are insulting every American out there to suggest that our country will become weak. We have the greatest military in history and nothing we will do will compromise our security.

Having said that, I want to replace wild spending with smart spending. The horrific waste by the Pentagon, the Department of Homeland Security, and other agencies involved in the effort to keep America impregnable is a matter of public record.

What is also a matter of public record is how the current legislators and those going back over two decades have refused to cut the pork, have toadied to the military-industrial complex, have been at the beck-and-call of corporate sponsors who lavish enormous amounts of cash on them in the form of campaign donations, and haven't seen a war they didn't love or a country exempt from America's relentless and senseless military expansion. We have nearly 1000 military bases in over 140 countries. There are only 196 countries in the world. I guess the Pentagon forgot to build bases on Tonga and in Andorra.

This is a vast waste of taxpayer money. As were the wars in Afghanistan and Iraq. There were no WMDs in Iraq. Osama bin Laden was on a dialysis machine in Kandahar, Afghanistan and the Taliban offered to turn him over to the U.S. Almost 3,000 of our young soldiers died supposedly chasing him around.

I will always stand strong for a strong America.

I will always also stand strong for a smart America.

Being smart doesn't preclude being strong.

Being smart means being stronger.

CHAPTER TWENTY-SIX

Going on the Offensive

While some progressives will be uncomfortable with it, there are times when it is absolutely essential, and will serve them admirably, to go on the offensive. To attack. To undercut the credibility of a reporter or media host, even a political opponent.

I only recommend this in certain very special situations, when to do otherwise will make a GP/I candidate look weak and afraid to do or talk about something which is clearly in the public interest.

Let me give an example.

The setup is this. A GP/I candidate running for president is challenged in a press conference by a New York Times reporter.

Q. There are reports floating around about irregularities in several states in terms of getting your name on the ballot. You say your campaign is based on honesty and openness. How can you claim the high moral ground when you seem to be subject to this kind of underhandedness?

A. There are reports floating about that there a planet invisible to us is in earth orbit, opposite the sun, and is inhabited by tarantula shaped faeries who dance like inebriated elephants. Anything I or my campaign has done is available for public scrutiny either in the public records, at our web site. Or it can be obtained by making a simple request to us.

Before I give you an answer to your specific question, let me make a more general comment about journalistic integrity.

You are with the New York Times, a newspaper which has long been called America's Newspaper of Record, widely acclaimed for objectivity and high reporting standards.

In 2002 in the lead up to the Iraq war, your paper passed along without any attempt at verification the lies the U.S. government was inventing to gain support for attacking Iraq. Your own Judith Miller aggressively supported completely bogus stories in support of that disastrous war. Ms. Miller was the head *pom-pom girl for <u>your</u> cheerleading team, which resulted in the destruction of a whole nation, the deaths of hundreds of thousands of innocent citizens and soldiers, the death of over 3,000 of our own fine men and women in uniform, and the creation of chaos and more death and suffering in the form of ISIS.*

That's just one example of such abysmal journalistic standards turning "America's Newspaper of Record" into a propaganda arm of the U.S. government.

So my answer to you is, I don't see what difference my answer to you would make. If you want an answer, just do what you normally do. Make something up that pleases the plutocrats, the corporate 1% who own your paper. I can't be bothered with shills who ask insulting and loaded questions which do not inform or benefit, and in fact mislead the American public, our good decent citizens who deserve real reporting on matters that really matter.

Next question?

At the risk of repeating a theme that has had a hammering previously in this book, let's talk about negativity.

If a person is dying of cancer and only has six months to live, is it negative for his doctor to tell him the awful truth?

It's certainly an unpleasant task.

But what would be negative is *not* telling the patient, not letting that person come to grips with their impending death, not allowing them to get their affairs in order, not allowing them to spend precious time with their loved ones in the quickly closing final chapter of life.

Telling the truth can be uncomfortable, even painful.

But it's never *negative*.

Often it's very positive, as when something good and constructive can come out of an ugly and unpleasant truth.

I want you to look objectively at the example I just gave.

Do you see what I see?

Do you agree about what is *truly* negative?

Letting some smug reporter *bait* the GP/I candidate is negative.

Letting these lying bastards continue to mislead the public is *truly* negative.

Letting them slide one more day for their prior sins is *irresponsible* and blatantly negative.

Keeping the public naive about the lack of journalistic integrity in even their most respected news sources is *unconscionable* and just plain wrong.

How can America function as a democracy if people are lied to and misled?

Let me be brutally frank here about what's in this for the GP/I candidate who called the smug New York Times reporter on the carpet for the abominable war record of his paper.

First, let me say, had the correspondent asked a sincere question which was not an ad hominem attack on the GP/I candidate, I would not suggest a counter-attack on him.

But his question was a classic *gotcha!* question. Clearly he was up to no good. He was just perpetuating the type of crude journalistic practice which the GP/I candidate accused his paper of, in one of the worst examples of jingoistic cheerleading by a respected major media organization in recent history.

Because it was such a cynical and confrontational question, and because light needed to be made of the abysmal journalism of the New York Times in its warmongering support for the Iraq War, and because this *fundamentally* supports the whole premise behind the war reparations invoice and the need for the Peace Dividend, this indeed was one of those "certain very special situations" where it was incumbent on the GP/I candidate to go on the attack.

So what's going to happen?

I won't predict how the Times will handle this.

But I know what the rest of the media will do.

This will be headline material.

[Name of GP/I Candidate] Rips Into New York Times
For Irresponsible Journalism

[Name of GP/I Candidate] Calls Out NYT for
Lies in Support of Iraq War

Judith Miller Attacked for Her Role in Bad
Reporting Leading Up to Iraq War

Even if six major corporations own all of the media in America, there is still some semblance of professional competition. MSNBC competes with Fox. CNN competes with both of them. The Washington Post competes with the New York Times. Fox competes with both of them.

Even though the New York Times would probably back-page this story, it is inconceivable that any of the other media outlets are going to let this one get away. Or risk being scooped by one of the other major MSM players, or worse, by some upstart like RT or the Huffington Post.

It'll be all over the news!

It'll certainly go viral on the internet.

Like I somewhat cynically said before, you can't buy advertising like this!

Most importantly, chipping away at both the official version of the news and the monoliths that peddle this propaganda directly reinforces the most essential elements of the GP/I candidate's message, especially the underlying premise of the Peace Dividend.

> *Folks, we've been lied to over and over.*
> *These wars are unnecessary and fraudulent.*
> *We have been deceived and screwed out of our tax dollars.*
> *Time for the piper to pay!*

• • •

It will always be a hard call when to go postal in a public setting.

A GP/I candidate cannot risk being judged surly or demented.

At the same time, opportunities which both serve the public interest *and* reinforce the GP/I candidate's message must always be used to best advantage.

If that means getting feisty and going on the offensive, so be it.

The unpleasant truth will out the wicked.

CHAPTER TWENTY-SEVEN

Bad Manners

Expect feigned shock and indignation from pundits and the major-parties alike when GP/I candidates come out swinging.

This can be used to phenomenal advantage.

Voters connect with straight talk, strong leaders.

Q. You are being criticized for being rude to your opponents, to interviewers, to resorting to negative campaigning. What do you say to that?

A. You call it rude. I call it frank. The American public wants straight talk, not polished-for-prime-time blather. The truth is not always pretty. I tell it like it is.

As for negative campaigning, you are very confused.

To call some one out on their lies is not negativity.
Their lies are the negativity.

To point to selfishness and greed is not negativity.
The selfishness and greed are the negativity.

To call a warmonger a warmonger is not negativity.
The sacrifice of innocent lives in unnecessary wars is the negativity.

The American people deserve leaders who will be honest, informed, direct to the point. Voters are adults. Looking at what has passed for leadership recently, sometimes the voters are the only real adults in the room. So I will continue talking to them like they're adults and treating them with the respect they deserve. And if the pundits and politicos act like misbehaving children, I will give <u>them</u> what they deserve.

CHAPTER TWENTY-EIGHT

Framing the Conversation

Notice a few things about all of the above answers.

The are assertive and unwavering.

They are unapologetic.

They are on-message.

They are not nuanced.

They are not attenuated.

They are simple and direct.

They are honest and steadfast.

They are pointed and unwavering.

Most importantly, they frame the discussion the way the GP/I wants it framed.

Remember, American voters are busy, distracted, impatient, and very suspicious.

Whether an answer is long or short, ideas must be bold, assertive, clear, simple. Voters don't hear complicated, wishy-washy, timid, half-way measures. They respect big ideas, smart ideas, forceful ideas.

It is not inappropriate or incorrect to use examples and metaphors which depart from the scholarly tracts where they ideas originated. It makes the message comprehensible.

We know that wealth distribution is embraced and posited by socialist thinkers. What's the point of going into that? People read the Bible a lot more than they read Marx and Engles. Talk to the people in terms they are familiar with and understand. Is this deceptive? Hardly. It's called good communication.

> *"Folks, it doesn't work when too few have too much. We can't have a strong America and a good future for our kids. Let's spread the love and let everyone get their fair share."*

Let the academics discuss the nuances. Let them argue over the genesis and evolution of the ideas. Let there be erudite and lengthy discussion which provides solid support and fully explicates every aspect of the ideas being promoted. But keep it in its place. It's not made for TV, it's not good for sound-bite news coverage, it sadly doesn't even fit in most public forums. Audiences are just too ADHD and stressed out now to concentrate on complex deliberations.

The point here is to give people a clear idea what the specific proposal is and why it works for them. If that means referencing the Bible, John Lennon, the Dalai Lama, Mickey Mouse, whoever, and doing that contributes to an honest, clear portrayal of the agenda, then that's what we do.

The goal is to communicate clearly and win elections.

And absolutely *vital* to success in connecting with the public is this:

We SHOULD NEVER let the right wing thugs manipulate perceptions by framing *anything* in their terms. We MUST assume control of the conversation at every available opportunity, shaping the public's perceptions in terms that are straightforward and clear, and in ways that are supportive of *our* agenda. *Never again* can we allow our ideas to be mocked and mutilated by malicious distortion. *Never again* can we allow the voting public to become victims of weapons of mass distraction and self-serving conceptual mayhem.

This is not just a priority for winning elections.

Honest and open national conversations are fundamental to sound democracy and a functioning society.

There's integrity and vitality in clear, honest communication. Lacking it is an invitation to extremes of confusion and demagoguery.

In politics that translates to anarchy and totalitarianism.

There is nothing in electoral politics more noble and rewarding than *connecting* with voters, sharing their concerns, values, aspirations, dreams.

There is nothing in a real democracy more intrinsically good and laudable, than a potential candidate's honestly deserving and winning the confidence and trust of voters, having that confidence and trust turned into a victory in the voting booth.

Epilogue

Feedback

Because I have had such an aggressively didactic style of writing, it's probably not all that apparent that I see this whole business of reforming electoral politics as a conversation. It's a conversation which has been sorely lacking and long overdue.

In this relatively brief manifesto, I have thrown my hat in the ring.

I'd like to think it's a good start.

Demanding legally binding commitments from prospective Senators, Congressman, even the President, bestows at least on specific issues a direct hand by citizens, tangible leverage as citizen/electors, a final say in some portion of the complex process of legislating and shaping our national landscape.

I would like to think that the detailed steps I have offered for introducing and implementing candidate contracts constitute a complete and sound strategy. But I recognize it is untested and may require many adjustments and improvements, fine-tuning in the workshop of real politics. I am certain it could also benefit from the advice of experts, open-minded individuals who have been in the trenches and may see areas where the strategy needs to be shored up against potential pitfalls, or augmented to overcome the inertia which typically cripples innovation.

The simple point I'm making is that while I don't think I have all of the answers, I hope I have injected enough into the discussion to get people thinking, excited, and motivated.

Frankly, during the last few years I have seen way too much pessimism and despair. If we as Americans truly take as much pride in our ingenuity and individual initiative as we say we do, the task of rescuing our democracy, no matter how daunting, is just another step in the long, ongoing process of perfecting the mechanisms of our experiment in self-government. We've made it through two world wars, the Great Depression, the Civil War, the Civil Rights Movement.

While the challenges we now confront are formidable, I believe electoral reform is still possible.

Perhaps you think my ideas are the ravings of a madman.

Or maybe you see some interesting, if flawed ideas.

Even better, you judge the bulk of the plan I've offered to be shovel-ready, and we just need to get to work.

Whatever the case, I would seriously like to hear your thoughts.

I'm not looking for just nifty compliments, stark condemnations, clever quips, or anything in between: 'Nice job, buddy!' 'Get a life, moron!' 'Stay in Japan.' 'Take fewer meds.' 'Kudos!'

Sorry. Empty comments of this sort, positive or negative, are not useful or welcome.

On the other hand, all constructive, thoughtful queries and recommendations are greatly appreciated.

john@jdrachel.com

Let's work together to move this forward. Nothing less than the survival of our country is at stake here. How could the penalty for failure or the reward for success be higher?

Addendum

I will close with something I put together for the blog page of my personal web site, published October 29, 2014. I believe it offers some good ideas and perspective, and overall embraces a sensible progressive world view.

• • •

"Ten Commandments for the New American Century"

First Commandment: THOU SHALT TAKE MONEY OUT OF POLITICS

No money in politics. Zero! First, people should stand up and declare unequivocally they will not vote for anyone who takes ANY money from corporations, lobbyists and PACs. Then, down the road, by having elections 100% financed out of public funds, we can build a democracy where our legislators might actually have some time to legislate. It is common knowledge, most federal office holders spend enormous amounts of time raising funds and worrying about winning the next election, instead of doing the job we voted them in office to do. Let's end this right now!

Second Commandment: THOU SHALT HONOR CHOICE AT THE POLLS

It's time to institute instant run-off, range or approval voting. This will allow minor party candidates to run at all levels of government without the understandable fear that a voter is throwing away her or his vote. Our current system has, as Ralph Nader has been saying all along, become a choice between Tweedle-dee and Tweedle-dum. Without real choice, meaning a range that covers the entire spectrum of political opinion, democracy becomes a sham, and purely an exercise in futility.

Third Commandment: THOU SHALT RESPECT THE COMMONS

Right off, we need to re-establish a commons. So much of what constitutes the foundation for a functioning society has been privatized — prisons, education, utilities, mail, roads, bridges. And it hasn't worked out well, has it? The nation's infrastructure is a shambles. There are some basic things we should all be able to have free and open access to, facilities and services which should not be at the mercy of the so-called free market: education, clean air and water, energy, health care, retirement security, the

INTERNET, police, fire and ambulance services, nutrition and mental health counseling. This is not socialism. It's having a country that works.

Fourth Commandment: THOU SHALT PUT MONEY CREATION AND THE CONTROL OF THE NATION'S CURRENCY BACK INTO THE PUBLIC DOMAIN

The control and issuance of currency must be returned to the federal government. The Federal Reserve is no more "federal" than Federal Express, and as a result America is now hostage to private banks and we are rapidly becoming their serf-slaves. Either nationalize or abolish the Federal Reserve and return creation of our fiat currency to the people of America, regulated by a legitimate, functioning system of representative government.

Fifth Commandment: THOU SHALT LIVE BY RULE OF LAW

We have a two-tiered legal system, a gentle one for the privileged, a brutal one for the rest of us. The oligarchs do what they want unfettered by pesky laws. Sometimes the same laws are used to restrain and incarcerate the rest of us. Same thing on an international level. Two tiers. The U.S. bullies the world, ignoring treaty obligations and international law, treating other countries as vassal states. But it uses the same legal instruments as a bludgeon, holding every other nation's feet to the fire with sanctions, UN resolutions, trade agreements — whatever — when it serves our interests, or more accurately, the interests of the corporations who are really setting the agenda. This gross hypocrisy is creating enemies everywhere. We are long overdue to again respect the law, apply it equally and fairly across the board, both at home and around the world.

Sixth Commandment: THOU SHALT REIN IN CAPITALISM

A nice breeze on a clear spring day — good! ... A Level 5 hurricane that destroys vast swaths of dwellings and kills countless people — bad! ... Surfer and swimmer-friendly waves lapping up on a sandy beach — good! ... A tsunami crushing whole towns with a 100 foot wall of terrifying force — bad! ... Sunlight from hydrogen fusion nurturing our planet with gentle rays of light and warmth — good! . . . An inferno of hydrogen fusion raining down on cities across the world as mammoth nuclear bombs, destroying the entire human race — bad! We mostly tend to agree that capitalism provides a powerful engine to drive development and progress. But too much of it and societies are crushed, democracies destroyed, vast numbers of people are relegated to serf status. Other countries have strict regulation and state control to check the ravaging effects of unfettered capitalism. Now it's America's turn. Either we rein it in or we can kiss good-bye our once-great country as it descends into the dustbin of history.

Seventh Commandment: THOU SHALT MAKE CORPORATIONS SERVANTS OF THE GREATER GOOD

It will be tough but the whole bogus concept of corporate personhood must be expunged. Totally voided. It was put in place by devious methods and now must be rooted out. In general, it's way past time to drastically restrict the charters of corporations, such that the interests of people are balanced with the pursuit of profit. This is the way it used to be in the early days of our nation. Back then, corporations were set up for specific and usually public-spirited projects, assigned a very narrowly defined charter and a fixed duration. When whatever was supposed to get done got done, the corporation was dissolved. Maybe we don't have to return to such a limited implementation in our modern world, but we do have to *require* that corporations serve the common good. It is entirely legal to dictate that corporations act responsibly and take into account the needs of the community they serve, especially the communities where they reside. We have to elect individuals who are not in the pockets of the corporations and have them re-write the laws for doing the business of America. If the multinational behemoths don't like it, let them set up in China, Vietnam or Bangladesh. That's where they already have their factories anyway. Ultimately this will not harm the economy. Rather it will create a society which is healthy and prosperous for *everyone*.

Eighth Commandment: THOU SHALT PROMOTE PEACE AND BE LOVED AGAIN

America must be taken off of a war footing. The high-alert status both at home and around the world is nothing more than highly destructive fear-mongering. It is used to promote a belligerent self-sabotaging approach to international relations. It's the product of a grossly delusional neocon imperialistic agenda which most Americans don't support — "exceptionalist" chest-beating which fills the coffers of the defense contractors but bankrupts the rest of us both financially and spiritually. We've meddled and bombed enough. It has accomplished nothing and created more problems and more enemies than we had before we decided that military force was the only way to deal with disagreements and crises in the world. It has also subjected the American people to unprecedented and unconstitutional levels of surveillance and a gross abrogation of our rights as citizens. Time to try peace and cooperation instead of threats and bullying.

Ninth Commandment: THOU SHALT RESPECT MOTHER EARTH

Enough silly arguing and tiptoeing around climate change. It's happening, it could destroy the human race. It will without a doubt reduce civilization to a shell of its former glory and sophistication. Let's get to work. Global warming and resource depletion represent the greatest threats to mankind in recorded history. Responsible use of resources and creation of sustainable sources of energy are not only necessary, but could be the greatest unifying force ever! Brainstorming and planning will create a monumental paradigm shift and the subsequent implementation of our collective ingenuity will create jobs and bring together behind a common purpose, a world which is torn by divisiveness, fear, suspicion, anger. Though time is quickly running out, the challenge of a planet in crisis doesn't have to end in total disaster. On the contrary, this could be a historic opportunity for a massive global initiative — one of renewal and fellowship.

Tenth Commandment: THOU SHALT LEVEL THE PLAYING FIELD

The rich and powerful have had a good run. The party is over. The wealthy should start paying back the country which gave birth to their monumental success. Inherited wealth does not give back to the community, the social and political environment that supported the accumulation of all that money. Tax it at 95% above $5 million. The heirs of the Koch brothers will just have to squeak by on their $5.2 billion. Capital gains? Capital gains *is* income. Tax it at the same rate as personal income. Speaking of which — time to return to the progressive tax rates of the 60s and 70s. You know them. The ones which resulted in a thriving economy! Massive tax reform across the board is in order, closing of all loopholes, penalizing off-shoring of profits, and the complete elimination of corporate welfare. Do I hear screaming of 'SOCIALISM!' out there? Get a life! Yes, this is *redistribution of wealth*. It's been going on for thousands of years. It's what makes a functioning society possible.

About The Author

John Rachel has a B.A. in Philosophy, is a novelist and established political blogger. He has written seven novels. His political pieces have appeared at OpEdNews, Russia Insider, Greanville Post, and other alternative media outlets.

Since leaving the U.S. in 2006, he has lived in and explored 31 countries. He is now somewhat rooted in a traditional, rural Japanese community about an hour from Osaka, where he lives with his wife of three years. Daily he rides his bicycle through the soybean fields and rice paddies which sprawl across the surrounding landscape. As of the date of the release of this book, he has a small but promising organic vegetable garden which begs his attention.

You can follow his writing and the evolution of his world view at:

http://jdrachel.com

Legal Notices and Disclaimers:

Candidate Contracts: Taking Back Our Democracy is an original work protected under international copyright law and registered with the U. S. Library of Congress © John D Rachel 2015.

The author acknowledges the trademarked status and trademark owners of any products referenced in this work, which have been used without permission. The publication/use of these trademarks is not authorized, associated with, or sponsored by the trademark owners, but appear as common and casual references in the context of presenting ideas, as they are common features in modern everyday life. No product endorsements are meant or implied by their use.

The author quoted a short segment of dialogue from the movie "Network", written by Paddy Chayefsky and directed by Sidney Lumet, distributed by Metro-Goldwyn-Mayer through United Artists, released November 27, 1976. All other appearances of similar quotations in this work are also attributed but used without permission.

www.ingramcontent.com/pod-product-compliance
Lightning Source LLC
Chambersburg PA
CBHW031202270326
41931CB00006B/371